PRAISE FOR PATRICIA WALSH
AND *BLIND AMBITION*

"We all have purpose and potential beyond what we can see or even imagine. In *Blind Ambition*, Patricia Walsh inspires you to take action immediately. She shows you how to identify your most important goals and then equips you to achieve them with her unique goal-attainment framework. Life's too short! Don't let another day pass without reading this book and beginning to apply her proven process."

—JEFF BOOHER, founder and CEO of TriDot.com and elite triathlon coach

"*Blind Ambition* demonstrates Patricia Walsh's ability to personally and professionally persevere while motivating others along the way. She helps you to understand the steps required to move beyond your daily challenges, eliminate excuses, and become your personal best to reach the goals you desire. If you are ready to put your life on a new course, read this book."

—JEREMY DRZAL, vice president of solutions management at Mozido

"An inspirational true story molded into a motivational tool . . . Patricia Walsh recognizes the heart of a champion in us all, and challenges readers to run through their limitations and toward their full potential."

—MEL GONZALES, assistant director of marketing at EBOOST

"Patricia Walsh is a transformational leader. Her distinct perspective, born of hard-won experience, is truly inspirational. This book is for those who want to be better leaders—or simply, better human beings."

—MICHAEL BISESI, professor at the Institute
of Public Service at Seattle University

"The struggles and triumphs that Patricia allows us to experience along with her in *Blind Ambition* are not just a testament to human potential, but a vision of what we are all capable of. There are few people in the world who can provide the motivation and vision of what is truly possible the way Patricia can. Regardless of what your goal may be or where you are headed, *Blind Ambition* will give you what you need to get there."

—ALEX AND CADEY CHARFEN, founders of the Charfen Institute

"People around Patricia Walsh always say that she ought to run around with a superhero cape around her shoulders, given everything that she manages to achieve. But as she shows in *Blind Ambition*, it is not some sort of innate ability that only a few people have (she wasn't born on the planet Krypton)—it is having goals and a method for achieving them. Patricia shares this method, her 'fuel, fire, blaze framework,' so that we can all run around with capes around our shoulders."

—TIAGO SOROMENHO, founder of StickyStreet.com and technology futurist

"For many people who are facing challenges in life or in business, it is easy to simply accept the reality that there are economic headwinds, that the competition is too tough, or that you just don't have what it takes to actually achieve success. It's ironic that Patricia Walsh's book can help you see your way past the obstacles that are in your way and achieve anything and everything that you want in life. Why ironic? Because Patricia Walsh is blind, which is supposed to be one of life's insurmountable obstacles. But when you read her book, it quickly becomes apparent that Patricia Walsh's vision will help to make you great!"

—BOB BABBITT, cofounder of the Challenged Athletes Foundation, cofounder of *Competitor* magazine, creator and host of Competitor Radio, creator of the Muddy Buddy Ride and Run Series, and member of the USA Triathlon and IRONMAN Triathlon Halls of Fame

"Patricia brings her passion and clarity to *Blind Ambition* to inspire and motivate readers. Don't wait. Read this book now and begin achieving your own life goals."

—SHARRON RUSH, executive director of Knowbility.org

"In *Blind Ambition*, Patricia Walsh shares her story and uses her unique experience, wit, and personality to show the reader that all goals are attainable if you have an action plan and a positive, can-do attitude. Her story will truly inspire you, and her action plan will challenge you to go after your own goals—no matter what the circumstances."

—NATASHA VAN DER MERWE, TriDot triathlon coach and professional triathlete

"At a time when the world is thirsting for people of deep and significant character, Patricia Walsh reminds us what a truly significant life looks like: fearlessly authentic and faithfully dedicated to improving the lives of others. In *Blind Ambition*, Walsh shares her fuel, fire, blaze framework, which has consistently placed her atop leaderboards. Her clear and actionable methodology will empower readers to be catalysts in their own lives."

—ANDREW WALSH, president and COO of Paint Sundries Solutions, Inc.

"In *Blind Ambition*, Ms. Walsh offers a fresh, powerful approach to attaining your goals. She encourages you to push beyond your perceived limitations, laying out an action plan that is both logical and approachable. *Blind Ambition* inspires and motivates you to forever change your perceptions of persons with disabilities—and yourselves."

—DR. GEORGEANNE FREEMAN, CEO of Downtown Doctor

"Patricia Walsh is a perfect example of what is possible. In *Blind Ambition*, Patricia conveys beautifully how to target and achieve your goals with an intensity and a focus that creates lasting change. Her story of her blindness as a child and her response to achieve her dreams is what it means to be human at its core."

—BEN SHOOK, PT, DPT, COMT, physical therapist

"If you are struggling with how you can set goals or fully unlock your own personal potential, *Blind Ambition* not only provides the framework for goal setting, but will help you discover your own ambition. Her inspiring story of loss, personal sacrifice, and starting over will leave you motivated to find your own sense of empowerment and meaningful contribution to the world."

—AMIE SMITH, owner of BlueDot Events

BLIND AMBITION

· · · · · · · · · · · · · · · ·

HOW TO ENVISION YOUR LIMITLESS POTENTIAL AND ACHIEVE THE SUCCESS YOU WANT

PATRICIA WALSH

New York Chicago San Francisco Athens London Madrid
Mexico City Milan New Delhi Singapore Sydney Toronto

1 2 3 4 5 6 7 8 9 0   DOC/DOC   1 2 0 9 8 7 6 5 4

ISBN   978-0-07-183382-0
MHID   0-07-183382-X

e-ISBN 978-0-07-183383-7
e-MHID   0-07-183383-8

McGraw-Hill Education books are available at special quantity discounts to use as premiums and sales promotions or for use in corporate training programs. To contact a representative, please visit the Contact Us pages at www.mhprofessional.com.

To Janet Patricia Munson, who proved to me that the right time to pursue your highest aspirations is today. It took tremendous bravery to start a career after keeping house for 20 years, and the students of Mount Si Middle School are fortunate that you did.

CONTENTS

ACKNOWLEDGMENTS

Thanks to Peter Economy for a great partnership in the writing of this book, and lending his expertise on the end-to-end publishing process. Your help made actualizing this dream possible, and I will forever be grateful for your hard work, your vision for success, and your enthusiasm for our shared dream of publication.

Thanks to John Gardner for setting an example of a person with a disability who was not defined by his lack of ability. It was your belief that you could change the world for the better that inspired me to reform myself and become an instigator of positive change. Thank you for seeing a spark of something that inspired you to include me in the Science Access Project and ViewPlus Technologies.

Thanks to all my professors in the electrical engineering and computer science and mathematics programs at Oregon State University. It took a village to get me through the demanding curriculum of an engineering college, and I will be forever grateful for the extra TA hours, the office hours, and your belief in my ability that set me loose in the world on a path to success.

Thank you to my leadership at Microsoft, including Steven Sinofsky, William Kennedy, Brian Utter, and Skip Backus. Having opportunities to succeed at Microsoft gave me a forum to prove to myself—and to others—that a person with blindness can make any meaningful contribution she sets her mind to. I hope to honor the lessons I learned in my time at Microsoft by disseminating to the world not only that a person with blindness can make a contribution, but that any person can achieve his highest aspirations by applying these lessons. There is no limit to what each of us can achieve. Thank you for betting on me and for cultivating my initial career success.

Thanks to the leadership at Mozido, including Felipe Fernandez, Teri Harwood, Randy Lund, and Emmert Ott, for having faith in my ability, affirming my belief that an organization can change the world for the better, and, above all else, rallying support when I faced adversity in the form of a family emergency and a parallel arson attack on my home. I will always deeply appreciate how all the employees of Mozido stood up and took action in my time of need.

Special thanks to the Challenged Athletes Foundation for providing me with opportunities to compete. I could not have trained and competed at the international level without your help and support. Thanks also to Nike, Rudy Project, PowerBar, Zico, Dodge, Ascenta, EBOOST, TriDot, Jack and Adam's Bicycles, teammac, and Pure Austin Fitness for your ongoing sponsorship. It is with your support that I have been able to exceed my own ambitions in the sport of triathlon.

Thanks to Natasha Van Der Merwe for pushing me hard, believing in my abilities, and leading by example. You work hard, so I follow. Thanks to Lilian Rincon for leading by example in dedication to your industry, the value in taking a risk, and the importance of bravery in career development. Having the opportunity to learn from you improved my confidence, my self-advocacy, and my belief that I, too, could be a leader in my industry.

Thanks to one of my dearest friends, Glen John, for being my sounding board and confidant. Thank you to Sandy Reifers and Shelly Barry for being with me in my darkest hour and for being my greatest supporters in my brightest hours.

Thanks to my little sister, Caitlin Richardson, for being my single greatest source of joy. You have grown up to be a brilliant, true-blue personality, and I couldn't be more proud. Thanks to Janet and David Munson for being my greatest source of unconditional support. Thanks to my cousin Andrew Walsh for being an example of how to successfully balance a thriving career and a happy family. Thank you for all your support over the years. I truly look up to you for good reason. Thanks to all my family and all my cousins. Your support over the years has filled me with gratitude. I feel only blessed by the genuine kindness, love, and sincerity with which I am surrounded, and I never question how fortunate I am to have such a strong clan behind me.

Last, but definitely not least, thanks to John Walsh for raising me to hold myself to a higher standard. I understand that no one knows exactly what to do when his child has special needs. The absolute strongest thing you did as a parent was to hold me to the same standard as any able-bodied peer. I am thankful always that you raised me to be self-sufficient, be resourceful, and live with no excuses.

INTRODUCTION

In my experience, people tend to view *blind* and *capable* as two mutually exclusive concepts. I live to disprove that notion. I live to be someone who transcends the expectation, someone who removes the qualifier. I am not good at what I do "for a blind girl"; I am simply good at what I do by *any* standard. I am willing to work harder, cultivate focus, and do whatever it takes to live to my full potential.

When people meet me for the first time, they often ask me why I carry a white cane meant for the blind when I'm able to see. If you were to encounter me randomly on the street or in a store or office, chances are you would assume that I could see as well as anyone else. None of my behaviors would lead you to believe otherwise. I don't rock back and forth. I don't stumble into things with my arms outstretched. I don't have a guide. Actually, I don't fit any of the social expectations of a person with blindness.

The truth is that I carry a white cane because I am unable to see—I am blind—and when people figure that out, they're often surprised. Why? Because I'm confident, together, and composed.

I've been blind since 1994. I can't see my hand at the end of my arm. Even the people I am around daily don't always realize how little I see. I have a six-degree tunnel of light, dark, and motion. If you're moving around, I'll probably get you, but if you're standing still, I'll miss you every time (this is why I really hate hanging plants). And while I am able to perceive whether a light is on or off, I cannot identify its origin, brightness, or color—only that it is on or off.

Blindness has certainly made accomplishing my goals more challenging, but I have never been stopped by my blindness. I hope to serve as an example of overcoming the common self-doubts that we all experience. I hope to serve as an example of defying learned helplessness in order to fulfill my potential. And, most important, I hope to serve as an example of the true power of goal attainment that is generated when you are being true to yourself in spite of any circumstances that might stand in your way.

While my blindness is a part of who I am, it does not define me, and it definitely does not keep me from achieving my goals. But I won't deny that my path in life has been a challenging one.

I was diagnosed with a pediatric brain tumor in 1986, when I was just five years old. While the surgeons were successful in removing the tumor, they also removed something else—about 75 percent of my vision. After the operation, I was completely blind in one eye and had about half of my vision remaining in the other eye. Because of lingering complications from the surgery, I lost the bulk of my residual vision at the age of 14—all but that six-degree tunnel of light, dark, and motion.

I sank into a deep depression. I was overweight, out of shape, and defeated. But there was a trail near my house, so I started running. Every day. The first time I ran a full mile, I was shocked that nothing bad had happened to me. The first time I ran eight miles, I was astonished at how far my legs could take me. The first time I ran a half marathon, I knew in no uncertain terms that this was no exercise in failure.

Learning to run changed my life. Through each incremental victory, I saw my hope for the future brighten. In the years since

I first took to that trail near my house, I have put myself through college, landed a job at Microsoft, run 12 full-length marathons, qualified for the Boston Marathon multiple times—making a lifelong dream come true—and completed two full-length IRONMAN competitions, crushing the world record for low-vision/blind male and female athletes. I have been the fastest woman on the U.S. paratriathlon team for three years running, and I am the current national and western hemisphere paratriathlon champion.

I have written this book so that you can understand and apply the same principles that I have learned from my many years of competing in the highest ranks of my sport and from working at the world's most successful software company. There has been a lot of trial and error along the way, but I have consistently set high goals, and I have consistently achieved them.

I present my unique fuel, fire, blaze approach to goal setting and show you how to apply it in your own job, career, and life. I explore each of the principles that support setting the highest goals, including defining your limits, being an iron man or iron woman, abiding the root line, not stopping until you cross the finish line, betting on yourself, living your core values, being resilient, and building willpower and goal-centric habits. I tell stories of how I applied each of these principles in my athletic career, in my work career, and in business, and I share lessons that readers can apply in their own work, career, and lives.

I hope you enjoy reading this book as much as I enjoyed writing it, and I hope that all your dreams—and your greatest goals—come true.

CHAPTER 1

MY BLIND AMBITION

· · · · · · · · · · · · · · ·

As long as I am breathing, in my eyes,
I am just beginning.

—Criss Jami

To me, blind ambition is a dedication to overcoming all the inevitable challenges that every one of us has to face if we are to exercise our full potential. It is an attachment to the idea that, despite your circumstances, you can realize your ambitions. It is the perception that no matter what the critics, naysayers, or Debbie Downers have to say about it, you are going to choose a limitless life. Blind ambition requires a relentless belief in yourself and a willingness to take risks from time to time.

There's a story I read as a child that has remained with me throughout my life. A woman trained for quite some time to swim the English Channel—accomplishing this challenging feat was her goal, her dream, and her obsession. Fewer people have made the 21-mile swim across the English Channel than have climbed Mount Everest! It takes an average of about 13 hours to complete the transit from the traditional starting point near Shakespeare's Cliff on the English coast to the finish at Cap Gris Nez in France. Not only does one have to be prepared to deal with powerful currents, winds, and waves—which force swimmers to zigzag across the Channel, adding grueling miles to the swim—but there are the stinging jellyfish, the clumps of leg-tangling seaweed, and the occasional plastic bag, bottle, or plank of wood. Not to mention the 600 or so tankers and 200 ferries, seacats, and other vessels that go through the Channel every day.

So the woman trained and prepared diligently for her attempt. Finally, the fateful day arrived. She donned her bathing suit, her goggles, and a thick layer of grease to protect her from the frigid water, and she began her swim. But despite months of preparation, the woman quit after just six miles—not even one-third of the way across the Channel.

Undaunted, she regrouped, devoted many more months to training, and made a second attempt. This time, she made it 12 miles before, dispirited and exhausted, she gave up.

The woman decided to pull out all the stops in preparing for her third attempt at conquering the Channel. She worked harder than she'd ever worked before, getting into the best possible physical and mental condition. She was certain that this would be her time—that victory would be hers.

And it very nearly was.

After swimming more than 20 miles in frosty water, battling formidable currents and stinging jellyfish, and dodging fast-moving ships and boats, she got to within 400 meters of the opposite shore.

And then she quit—exhausted and defeated.

But why did she quit? She was only 400 meters away from achieving the goal that had consumed her for so many years.

Tragically, as the swimmer neared the shore, a thick fog enveloped her, and she became disoriented—blind to her surroundings. And because she couldn't see the approaching shore, she didn't know how close she was to achieving her goal. With the ability to see taken away from her, she could just as easily have been 400 miles away from her goal as the 400 meters that she actually was. Overcome with fatigue and uncertainty, the woman gave up, climbed into her rescue boat, and took what turned out to be a very short ride to shore. It was only then that she realized her heartbreaking error.

The limitation that she felt because of her disorientation was a *perceived* limitation. She undoubtedly could have completed the final 400 meters of her swim if she had realized just how close she was to her goal. The conditions eroded her psychological belief in her own abilities. Unable to see her surroundings, she was faced with a choice of believing that her goal was possible or believing that it was impossible. She chose impossible.

My heart aches for her, as I know she must have been at a breaking point. To choose to see the unknown as possible takes deliberate training. When things are overwhelming—when I'm running a race or taking on a particularly difficult project at work—I tell myself often that the shore is just 400 meters away. From her tragic example, I learned to assume that fulfilling your dreams is within your grasp. Stay focused in the moment. Prepare and practice some awareness of what the pursuit means to you.

I keep this story at the back of my mind for those times in my life when quitting seems to be the only option—when I'm beyond exhaustion, when pain racks my body, and when everything within me is screaming for me to stop. When I find myself at the end of the rope and about to let go, I remind myself of this story. I know that, although I can't see through the fog that permanently envelopes me, my goal is within reach. I just need to push away the doubts, ignore the pain and exhaustion, and keep my focus on forward motion.

The truth is, we all struggle with blindness. None of us knows what will happen next in our lives, our work, and our careers. We all are enveloped in some sort of fog. The outcomes are always unclear, and victory is never certain until we cross the finish line. We all struggle with doubts, negative experiences, and incomplete information. But if we are to achieve the goals we set for ourselves, we must ignore the noise and push ourselves ever forward until we accomplish what we set out to do.

I was born in 1981 in Port Angeles, Washington, to John Walsh and Linda Richardson. My dad kept an old Jeep in our yard, and I used to roll down the window of the parked car and try to leap in through the window, *Dukes of Hazzard* style. Unfortunately, I never quite made the jump; in fact, I regularly hurt myself in my attempts. But that minor detail didn't stop me from trying again and again. I figured that the error in my approach was my height, so I added a small mini-cooler as an interim jump. I leapt from the ground to the mini-cooler, then made one more leap that I was certain would place me squarely through the open window of the Jeep.

I was wrong, and more injuries followed. I later came to call this sort of persistence a willingness to fail gracefully. At the time, I really just loved the idea of leaping into a car and speeding away. And I often felt like speeding away after my parents divorced in April 1986. No divorce is easy, but my parents' divorce was particularly tumultuous. I bounced around the homes of different friends and relatives for some time.

A few months after the divorce, while we were riding a ferry across Puget Sound, my dad and my sister expressed excitement at seeing a seal swimming alongside our boat—at least, that's what they tried to convince me was happening. I was used to my dad's jokes, so I didn't think anything of it. I knew there was no seal in sight. They had conspired to play a trick on me. I stubbornly argued that there was no seal, and that I wasn't going to be fooled that day. But in fact, there was a seal about 50 yards from the boat. It was at that moment that my dad first realized that there was something wrong with my vision.

Dad took the precautionary step of taking me to a local eye doctor. I think he assumed that it would be a quick fix. Maybe I'd enter kindergarten with Coke-bottle glasses. He had no sense of the severity of the situation.

The doctor diagnosed the problem: I had a "lazy" right eye. He recommended that I wear a patch over my left eye, the one that the doctor said was normal. It was meant to force the lazy eye to work harder to compensate for the covered eye, strengthening it in the process. What the doctor did not realize, however, was that I could not see out of my right eye at all, so putting a patch over my left eye left me completely blind. I adapted quickly to this new, dark world into which I had been thrust: I learned to tell the Ninja Turtles apart by their voices. Telling the voices of the Transformers apart was far more complicated, but with time and effort, I could eventually identify the vehicles. More than meets the eye is an understatement.

The doctor soon realized that the patch wasn't helping, but he said that there was nothing more he could do. We went to a different doctor, who explained to my dad that I was faking the vision problem in a bid for attention. Port Angeles is a small town, and everyone in the community was aware of the tumultuous divorce that my parents had gone through. So the doctor decided to play psychologist, combining the rumors he had heard about our family with the behavior that I was exhibiting to arrive at his diagnosis. There I was, a partially blind five-year-old, being told in the examination room by this doctor that all I was suffering from was a need for attention.

All I remember after that is Dad ushering me out of the room. As I sat in the hallway, I heard him yelling at the doctor. Soon after, he made an appointment with an eye doctor in Seattle. I took a Tuesday off from kindergarten, and we made the trip into the city. The doctor examined my optic nerves by dilating my eyes and using a special scope. When he looked into my right eye, he saw that the nerve was gray. It should have been pink. The eye doctor immediately knew that I was blind in my right eye. The examination showed that I *could* see out of my left eye, but not very well.

Everything happened quickly from there on. The doctor scheduled an emergency MRI for that Thursday. The MRI revealed that I had an advanced brain tumor the size of a golf ball, and surgery was scheduled immediately. On the day of the surgery, I was rolled down the hospital hallway to the operating room, with nurses and doctors trying to comfort me all along the way. I remember being surrounded by unfamiliar faces while fluorescent lights flickered by on the ceiling like a time-lapse movie.

After surgery, the nurses slowly woke me up in a recovery room. There had been damage to my pituitary gland, a small organ (about the size of a pea) attached to and located just below the hypothalamus. One of the jobs of the hypothalamus is to keep our bodies in homeostasis, which means keeping vital processes such as body temperature, pH, water, and electrolytes in balance. This caused me to feel like I was dying of thirst, even if I had just had a drink of water. They fed me ice chips, but nothing could alleviate my intense thirst. As a five-year-old, I didn't understand any of this. I was still restrained in my hospital bed, and when a nurse placed a piece of ice in my mouth I bit her out of frustration. I was a sick, traumatized, thirsty kid—reduced to animal instincts.

My vision had been reduced to a tunnel out of my left eye. I could see clearly within this narrow tunnel, but I had no peripheral vision at all. I could see something only if it was relatively close or immediately in front of me. I could recognize a face if it was within five feet of me, but if it was any farther away, the images quickly went out of focus and grew fuzzy. I used to compare tunnel vision to looking through a paper towel roll. You can see only what is on the other end, not what's on either side. It's like having blinders on.

After I was released from the hospital, it suddenly became clear to me that I was different from the other children I knew. It increasingly bothered me when anyone tried to make too much of a point of it. I didn't like being segregated in classes, and I hated it when the teacher gave me a separate activity in physical education. The other kids would be playing basketball while I sat on the sidelines, stacking blocks or doing some other activity that was more suitable for a toddler. Even at such a young age, I knew how patronizing and condescending this was. I was born ambitious, and I immediately felt that I was a second-class citizen. I hated feeling less than.

My vision remained steady at 20/600 until 1994. At the age of 13, because of some complications with my medication and post-operative scarring, I lost the rest of my vision—in a single day. The problem was damaged nerve tissue, not a defect of my eye. This is why I don't look blind. My right eye tracks correctly when people talk, and I've been told on numerous occasions that I look right at people. This is strange because it is my right eye that is completely blind. My left eye, however, has a mind of its own and travels the world. It can be pointing in any direction at any given time, and it is the eye that I see some light out of.

Before I lost my vision completely, my plan had been to graduate early from high school—not just to gain early admission to college, but also to escape the anger within my family that I had endured as I was growing up. I knew that college was going to be my ticket to a better life, so I worked hard at my studies. I won statewide essay contests, and I took tests to fast-track math—all with the intent of moving ahead quickly and building my résumé for college. The work paid off. I was able to skip sixth-, seventh-, and eighth-grade math, and I was on track to graduate at the age of 16.

But once I lost my vision, I felt as if all my opportunities were over. I went from being at the top of my high school class to struggling to read "See Jane run" in Braille. My aptitude for math had gone down in flames, and I was convinced that every shred of my potential had been destroyed in the inferno. My hope for my own future was dim. I didn't understand the tools or the technology that would help me through this difficult time. All I had was a bottomless pit of grief for all my lost potential. I thought I was doomed to sit on the sidelines forever, stacking blocks for the rest of my life, while other kids went on to higher education, careers, and successful lives.

Before I lost my vision completely, I had read the Richard Leakey *Origins* books, and I wanted to be a paleoanthropologist. But after losing my vision, I had no idea what I would do. The School for the Blind had once taken us on a career day to observe blind people at work, and I was immediately struck by the fact that all the people we visited that day had notably underwhelming careers. One woman worked two hours a day at an office. During those two hours, she answered the phone and dictated messages to the receptionist. She had no real responsibility—the company had hired her as a favor, and it coddled her to make her feel useful. As a 14-year-old, I could see that my future had been reduced to a feel-good kind of contribution. That prospect shattered my sense of self on so many levels.

Learning Braille proved to be difficult, so I wasted day after day, immersed in the heartache of my lost future. I sank into despair, and I used cigarettes, alcohol, and drugs to try to numb the pain. In hindsight, I was actually quite busy—I was teaching myself to be helpless. I had received so much discouragement that I started to believe in and internalize my helplessness. I was convinced that my efforts would end in failure, so on the few occasions when I decided to do something positive with my life, I would sabotage my own efforts. And every failed attempt only reinforced my belief in what I could *not* do. I was the originator and perpetuator of my own learned helplessness.

My lack of hope led me on a broken road. I was constantly defying authority. As far as I was concerned, my life was over, so I made no attempt to hide the fact that I was no longer trying. After having been suspended five times for an assortment of smoking and drinking violations, I was expelled from the Washington State School for the Blind in the ninth grade for bringing an assortment of drugs to school.

When the school refused to take me back, I moved with my dad to a house in northern Ontario, Canada. Actually, to call the place we moved into a house is an exaggeration. In reality, it was a summer cottage with no heating system. It was never intended for people to live in year-round—but we did. Thankfully, my dad has absolutely zero tolerance for any whining or self-pity. He worked in the wood products industry. We moved to Canada because all the environmental legislation in the United States in the mid-1980s had resulted in changes in logging practices that shrank the U.S. wood products industry and slashed the number of available jobs.

After our move, I decided that I wanted to learn to play baseball. My dad took a lot of heat from the neighbors for repeatedly throwing baseballs at my face. I never did manage to catch them with only auditory clues, but I always appreciated his willingness to try. While this was a painful exercise, it helped me cultivate quick reflexes in spite of my vision loss. I sustained a few black eyes along the way, but in the process, I learned that I was simply not that fragile. Getting hurt is part of life, and even if I never caught a ball, every once in a while I came close, and that was exciting. These moments of normalcy helped me see myself as not so different from the rest of my peers.

I enrolled in a regular local high school—the W.C. Eaket Secondary School in Blind River, Ontario. My sophomore year, I felt as if I was taking one step forward and two steps back. My ambition flickered in the darkness of my hopelessness, but my old friend had turned into a devil on my shoulder, taunting me about everything that could have been but now never would be. It left me deeply conflicted and in emotional turmoil.

When Dad and I had the typical conflicts that a teenage daughter and a single father are bound to have, he would always talk to me about the issue—directly and without beating around the bush. Dad can have a quick jab in his wit, but he isn't one to yell. I responded well to his direct communication, and I was always honest with him in return—for better or for worse. He helped me get services from the school, and I started to learn Braille math and how to use some of the available computer systems and Braille note-taking devices.

My turnaround began to gain momentum. I had a vision of a better self, and I began to realize that I could and should start setting some goals for myself. I felt a deep-seated desire to lift up my life, but my behavior was still all over the map. I would enroll in an advanced class, prove that I had some aptitude, and then check out for a while. I would make these periodic attempts at something better. I knew I was capable, but I felt blocked at every turn by the tragic circumstances that weighed me down.

I had only a few real friends in high school, and I had become a bit of an outcast. I wanted to make more friends, and there were a variety of clubs, sports, and other activities for me to choose from. I decided to join the track team, which at the time had only about five or six people. I liked the idea of doing something active and something that I could do outside. Football and basketball were out of the question, so track it was. This was my first opportunity to relate to my peers in something I was capable of doing. It took several crashes, but eventually I learned to trace the outer edge of our sand track. Once I learned how to clear the track, I then trained to improve.

I ran on the sand track behind our small school, and it was the first time that I started feeling a hint of the aptitude that I had felt before I lost my vision completely. My track team was positive and encouraging. I felt for the first time that I had made some real friends in Ontario. I felt for the first time that I had peers based in some common interest that was positive. I had allowed my self-image to become dull and tarnished, and engaging with peers was a step toward helping my self-image shine.

But, as I soon discovered, not everyone was going to be anxious to help me in my journey to significance.

I had competed against sighted girls in all the various regional and district races with no problem. This changed, however, when I was slated to compete at the provincial level at the annual Ontario Federal Secondary Association track meet. Unexpectedly, some higher-up decided that there would be an issue of liability if I ran the race. They weren't worried about *my* getting hurt, however. They were worried that I was going to be a danger to the *other* girls. I ran on the inside lane, and I kept myself on course by keeping the edge of the inside lane under my foot. I could feel the difference, and I knew where I should be. I had never run into another girl on the course, and there was no reason to believe that all of a sudden I would.

Fortunately, some local attorneys in the Blind River community stood up and helped me fight the new restrictions, and I was allowed to compete in the 100-meter sprint. I won the race, earning my first gold medal and gaining a huge dose of self-confidence.

I realized that college was a very real possibility, and I set my sights on that goal. I knew that if I stayed in Canada, there was no way I would be able to afford the nonresident tuition, so I moved back to the United States and into my mom's house, against my dad's wishes. My intention was to establish residency and gain eligibility for in-state tuition.

I enrolled in Snohomish High School, northeast of Seattle. I needed to save money for college, so I worked as many hours at McDonald's and Taco Bell as I was legally allowed to as a minor. Sometimes I actually worked more hours than were legally allowed by working two jobs at once, plus I had occasional side jobs for a contractor. This meant that I didn't have time for extracurricular activities. I had to stop running—there just weren't enough hours in a day. I was averaging more than 30 hours a week on the job, while doing what I could to bring my grades back up and prepping for college-entrance exams.

Fortunately, all this hard work paid off and I was able to manage a good enough SAT score and improve my GPA enough to earn acceptance at Oregon State University.

Success!

Despite my achieving this momentous goal, the challenges continued. My mom and stepdad were under the mistaken impression that every blind student in the state of Washington received tuition grants. As a result, they refused to fill out the FAFSA form, which is required by U.S. universities and colleges to determine eligibility for scholarships. I ended up stuck with out-of-state tuition and no financial support from my family, nor from the many scholarships that I had to give up because of the lack of financial information. I was carrying a full course load of studies and working the 2:00 a.m. to 10:00 a.m. shift at a local 24-hour breakfast joint. Despite this, I was able to make it through five terms of study before I was forced to take a break from school because of the mounting financial pressures.

But my life was about to take a dramatic turn for the better.

While I was at OSU, I learned of a blind physics professor—Dr. John Gardner—who was working on an innovative science-math-engineering educational curriculum for the blind. In spring 2000, I found my way to his office and introduced myself.

I may not have used the term at the time, but I was a huge believer in the "fake it until you make it" principle. The professor asked me about my computer skills, and I exaggerated dramatically. The only thing that had any real basis in fact at the time was that I had become a decent Braille math reader. He hired me as tech support (which was insane) and Braille proofreader. That evening, I went home and ungraciously demanded that a roommate teach me how to use e-mail, which was a key skill for tech support. Until then, I had not embraced technology.

Despite the fact that I was on an upward trajectory, I was still operating in survival mode. I was worried about my future every minute of every day. I felt as if I didn't have any support, and for the most part I didn't. Everyone thought my pursuit of higher education would end in failure, and they were all pretty open about voicing their opinions. I felt like that little kid on the sidelines who had no business being in the game. I was still a smoker, and as a result of my crazy school and work schedule, I was out of shape and overweight. While I was on the right track at school and at work, I knew that I would have to do something to turn around my deteriorating physical condition.

I started running again.

There was a trail near my house, and again I ran by tracing the inside line with my foot. The only problem was that I could never figure out how to get back home. But that minor inconvenience didn't slow me down. I ran every day, leaving a rock or something else for myself to indicate when I had returned. I'd run out and back on the same trail, adding a little more distance each time. If all went well, the rock I had left for myself would trip me on the way back. Crashing was part of the plan. That's how I knew that I needed to get off the trail and head home. The first time I ran a full mile, I was in shock that nothing bad had happened to me.

Once again, running had changed my life for the better—just as it had when I experienced some measure of success on my high school track team in Canada. Slowly but surely, my physical health improved, which motivated me to clean up my diet. And after trying every nicotine patch and gum product on the market, I was finally able to kick the smoking habit once and for all.

I continued to run, adding distance with each outing and becoming stronger and more confident in my abilities. In spring 2000, I ran my first half marathon, and six months later, I ran my first full marathon. When I achieved this milestone, I knew for the first time that my efforts were not the exercise in futility that so many people had told me my life would be.

In addition to the personal satisfaction I felt from proving to myself that I could achieve this goal, I relished the opportunity to prove my naysayers wrong. The best revenge is a life well lived. I felt a renewed hope and a sense of power. The world was again my oyster—I had a future after all. I knew that I would always have a steeper learning curve, and that I would always have to work a little harder than everyone else to achieve my goals. But I knew that I held the reins to my future in my hands, and that I would determine my ultimate success or failure. I felt that my future was bright. I felt that I could fulfill my ambition and the potential that I had given up when I lost my vision. I felt a renewed sense of all that is possible.

I took two years off from my university studies to work for John Gardner and the Science Access Project, which gave me the opportunity to develop key professional skills, learn technology, and make a meaningful contribution. Along with the rest of John's team, we helped build what eventually became ViewPlus Technologies, the developers of the Tiger tactile graphics and Braille embosser. John and his wife, Carolyn Gardner, embraced me like family. They helped me navigate the financial aid system so that I could be declared financially independent and would be eligible for the scholarships that were available to me.

Having a role model like John Gardner, who was blind, but was capable of changing the situation for persons with disabilities, had a remarkable impact on my future. The example he set stoked the flicker of hope that was burning within me. I loved working for him and his family. I took tremendous pride in being part of something bigger. I felt capable. I felt talented. I felt that I was good at what I did. The mounting pride helped me over all the hurdles that were yet to come.

While I was working for ViewPlus, I discovered that I had an aptitude for public speaking and making presentations. I learned how to put together PowerPoint presentations on the company's products, and I presented them all over the country. After one such presentation, a woman whom I had never met before—or since—pulled me aside and asked me what it was like being a blind woman in engineering. The fact that she thought it was possible for me to be in engineering floored me.

But this random interaction caused me to reevaluate my life.

In the fall of 2002, I reenrolled at OSU, this time in computer science. Even John Gardner, God bless him, pulled me aside and told me that he didn't think computer science was for me. Again I was flooded with messages telling me that this path I had chosen for myself was fated to be an exercise in failure. But I wasn't so sure—I knew it could go either way. I had developed basic tech skills, but nothing advanced. I knew that I'd be behind the others in my class and that I'd be at a disadvantage on many levels. But I had a burning desire to know what I was capable of. I knew that even if it didn't work out, I'd be better off for having made the attempt. I knew that I would rather fail gracefully than wonder for the rest of my life about what might have been.

I barely passed my first term. I knew I wasn't ready. I spoke with my professors, and they all tried to talk me into going into similar, but less technical fields. I knew that my attempt could be an exercise in failure. I knew that I might just be proving all the naysayers right. I wasn't worried about proving them right; I was worried that they *were* right. I was desperate to hold on. My hope for the realization of my vision of a better self hung in the balance. My intense desire to excel in engineering was intended to prove my ability to myself. I fought desperately to stay in the game.

I dug in my heels, and I found every tutoring service at Oregon State University and in the city of Corvallis. I frequented each professor's office hours at every available opportunity. When you've been spoon-fed ideas about what you are not capable of all your life, reaching out for help makes you feel like a failure. It hits that same nerve that is raw from defeat. I knew that if I was to stand any chance whatsoever, I was going to have to use every tool in the toolbox, and that would include asking for help. If asking for help didn't work, I was going to have to beg for help. Before every tutoring session, I felt anxiety. I felt as if I was certain to be the stupidest pupil the tutor had ever worked with in his life. I could see myself being laughed out of the offices. Truthfully, some professors and TAs did treat me that way. They didn't understand my vision problems, and I was constantly playing catch-up. Overcoming my unwillingness to ask for help and dealing with all the punches to my ego along the way was grueling—often more grueling than the curriculum. It felt like I was being beaten down and responding immediately with, "May I have another?"

After endless hours of persistent questions, my professors started to warm up to the idea.

Eventually, I proved to my professors that I wasn't going anywhere.

After my second term, when I again passed by just slightly less than the skin of my teeth, my professors had a change of heart. Once they figured out that I wasn't going to budge, they all started adding extra hours for me. Some even helped me in their homes on evenings and weekends. I spent Thanksgiving and holidays with my professors. Some had TAs assigned to assist me in lectures and work with me one on one. I lasted through the advanced math and physics. I held my own in the electrical engineering courses. In a field that was 97 percent men and just 3 percent women, I had survived in one piece. By the end of my program, I was not at the top of my class, but I was in the high middle.

When it came time for my professors to make recommendations to companies like Microsoft and Google, I turned up on several short lists. The same professors who had once tried to detour me away from the computer science program were now recommending me to the nation's top information technology firms.

Microsoft offered me a job, and I proudly accepted it.

As I accepted my job offer, I thought back for a second and realized that only a few years earlier, I had considered a fast-food job to be a miracle. In accepting a position at one of the leading technology companies, I felt as if I had moved a mountain. This was the beginning of a new paradigm in my life. Previously, I had been forced to fight for scraps. Now I felt that I had some say in my future. I had aptitude. I had the potential not only to live out the vision I had for a better self, but also perhaps to exceed that vision.

Since that momentous day, I have achieved many more accomplishments in my life. I founded my own company, Blind Ambition, and I started working as an engineer at the Austin-based software company Mozido. In the years since I first took to that trail near my house, I have completed 12 full-length marathons, qualified for the Boston Marathon multiple times—making a lifelong dream come true—and completed two full-length IRONMAN competitions, crushing the world record for low-vision/blind male and female athletes. I have been the fastest woman on the U.S. paratriathlon team for three years running, and I am the current national and Western Hemisphere paratriathlon champion. I am proud of how far I have come, but I also feel that I am just getting started.

From where I stand now, I feel that I have only one option, and that is to do everything possible to help others feel the same sense of empowerment that I do, and to help others learn how to apply the lessons that I have learned in setting and achieving goals against what sometimes seem like insurmountable odds. This involves the fuel, fire, blaze goal hierarchy. Your challenges may not look the same as mine, but they will challenge you in the very same way. I hope my experience provides you with the tools you need to overcome all the barriers between you and your highest aspirations.

• • • Lessons • • •

During the course of your life, you are going to constantly encounter and have to deal with people who will tell you to your face (and even more often behind your back) that you don't have the smarts, the talent, the experience, or whatever else it might take to succeed at something that you've set your sights on achieving. *Naysayers* are the people who try to cut you down to size loudly and overtly—they don't hide their intentions. *Discouragers* are much more subtle in their approach: they plant small seeds of doubt within you, and then water them and hope they'll grow.

It's important to let the naysayers know that you are aware of the game they are engaged in, and that you aren't interested in playing. Similarly, you need to let the discouragers know that you aren't buying what they are trying to sell you. Here are some specific tips for dealing with the naysayers and the discouragers in your life.

- Take the warnings you receive from others with a grain of salt.
- Decide for yourself. You have your very own brain and the ability to make up your own mind.
- Don't show anger. Showing anger demonstrates to the naysayers and discouragers that their strategy is working.
- Listen to your own inner voice and ignore those who say that you can't do what you know you can.
- Prove the naysayers and discouragers wrong—over and over again.
- If you cannot turn them into supporters, then work the naysayers and discouragers out of your life. Surround yourself with supporters, motivators, and mentors.

CHAPTER 2

FUEL, FIRE, BLAZE

· · · · · · · · · · · · · · ·

I WOULD RATHER BE ASHES THAN DUST!
I WOULD RATHER THAT MY SPARK SHOULD
BURN OUT IN A BRILLIANT BLAZE THAN
IT SHOULD BE STIFLED BY DRY ROT.
I WOULD RATHER BE A SUPERB METEOR,
EVERY ATOM OF ME IN MAGNIFICENT
GLOW, THAN A SLEEPY AND PERMANENT
PLANET. THE PROPER FUNCTION OF
MAN IS TO LIVE, NOT TO EXIST. I SHALL
NOT WASTE MY DAYS IN TRYING TO
PROLONG THEM. I SHALL USE MY TIME.

—Jack London

I t doesn't matter whether I'm talking with a group of CEOs or an auditorium full of sixth graders. The most common question I am asked, regardless of the audience, is how I maintain my drive during the days, weeks, and months leading up to a competition, and then how I carry that drive through to the finish line. After hearing this question asked repeatedly by all kinds of audiences, I realized that, regardless of their age, social status, or career path, people are hungry for the tools they need if they are to achieve their ambitions. My answer to the question is actually quite simple and straightforward: I dream big dreams, and then I create the goals that enable me to make them real.

A fire can be practically invisible (for example, the pinpoint flame of a miniature welding torch), or it can be overwhelmingly obvious, like a massive forest fire that engulfs acre after acre in its path. At its very core, a fire is a chemical chain reaction that occurs when fuel, heat, and an oxidizing agent (such as oxygen) are combined, and this chain reaction can be explosive and very powerful.

To me, goals are a chain reaction of sorts, more mental than physical, and the results of achieving the goals that you set can be explosive and very powerful in your own life. The fuel for my goals is my determination to follow through; my fire comes from my desire to achieve; my blaze comprises my highest-level goals, of which I have many. One of these highest-level goals is my sincere hope of changing the perception of persons with disabilities, so that the expectation is that they will lead the pack. Another is my desire to represent the United States in the 2016 Paralympics in Rio de Janeiro. And yet another is to become an accomplished software engineer in a fast-growing company.

In this chapter, I will explain the power produced by setting ambitious goals.

WHAT DRIVES ME FORWARD

When you watch an athletic competition, whether in person or on television, you are witnessing an event that is exciting for participants and audience alike. Hearts are pumping, muscles are straining, and adrenalin is surging. Depending on the particular event, the competition may be over within seconds (Usain Bolt won the 100-meter sprint at the 2012 Olympics in just 9.63 seconds), or it may take hours (the record for the IRONMAN Hawaii triathlon is a few minutes over eight hours) or even days (the 3,000+-mile-long Race Across America ultramarathon bike race takes its winners eight or nine days to complete, depending on conditions). While the surge of excitement that drives participants forward in a competition and pushes them to give their all is easy for anyone to see during the course of the event, what you don't see are the many days, weeks, and months of tedious practice, early morning workouts, and other training routines that enable a high-level athlete to compete against the best in the sport. It's really here that races are won—in the gym, on the road, or in the water, day after day, week after week, month after month, and year after year. Races are won by making a high-quality, focused effort over time, developing key skills, and putting in the time needed to allow for adaptation.

There is plenty of scientific research that clearly demonstrates the power of setting goals. In a study of 38 individual research studies on group goal setting published in the *Journal of Applied Psychology* in 2011, researchers reported that they had found three characteristics of performance-boosting group goals:

1. *Specific.* Goals that are precisely defined result in significantly higher levels of performance than goals that are vague. So, for example, the goal "Earn a score of

'outstanding' at our next team performance appraisal" will drive higher levels of performance than the less definite goal "Do a better job executing all of our work duties."

2. *Difficult.* When you shoot for higher goals—goals that are more difficult to achieve—you will deliver higher levels of performance as you work to attain them. According to research, stretch goals—where you have to stretch to attain a goal, but not so much that the goal is impossible to reach—are best. A stretch goal on the job might be, "To increase overall customer satisfaction ratings by 10 percent in the next three months," where a 5 percent increase might be more typical.

3. *Group-centric.* When people are working in a group situation, the researchers found, only individual goals that were group-centric—that is, that maximized individuals' contributions to the group—improved performance. Individual goals that were egocentric—that is, that were focused on maximizing personal performance at the expense of the group—decreased group performance.[1]

In another study of business-related goal setting, Dr. Gail Matthews, a psychology professor at Dominican University of California, found that people who write down their goals and then share them with a friend are much more likely to accomplish them. According to Matthews, people who simply thought about the goals they hoped to achieve within a four-week period of time accomplished those goals only 43 percent of the time. However, people who wrote down their goals, shared them with a friend, and took the extra step of sending that friend a weekly progress report achieved an astounding 76 percent of their goals.[2]

People often assume that I am personally motivated through some innate—perhaps even animal—competitive drive. The truth (as hard as it might be to believe) is that I'm not an inherently competitive person. In my heart, winning is neither here nor there—it's not what drives me forward. Instead, I am motivated by my knowledge that I can personally have a powerful and, I hope, lasting impact on the way people view individuals with a disability. I am driven to be a catalyst—a chemical that facilitates a chain reaction—that will cause people in the future to see an individual with a disability and expect her to be a high achiever.

When I am congratulated for successfully crossing the street independently, something that almost anyone can do without much difficulty, I have to admit that I am offended. Why? Because sighted people are continually surprised to see that I am competent, surprised to see that I am a capable adult, and surprised to see me flourish. In my perfect world, no one should be surprised to find that I am just as capable as he is. I hope to be a catalyst for the creation of a new worldview in which the average person won't see me as different and won't be surprised that I can do the same things he can. If winning races is the best avenue for me to use to accomplish that goal, then I will dedicate my whole self to winning races.

One of my highest-level goals is to be a catalyst for change in the athletic industry. I want to set the bar so high that for generations to come, athletes with disabilities will be competing in an environment where there are greatly improved opportunities for athletic sponsorship, scholarship, and success.

When I lost my vision, I lost more than the ability to see. I lost my sense of self-worth. I was convinced that my blindness made me damaged goods and that I could no longer contribute anything to the world. As I found success in running marathons, however, I woke up to the fact that I had so much left to give. I no longer felt that I had to prove anything to anyone, and I was free to explore my interests, wherever they might take me. I had commenced an upward trajectory in my life, and my new mission was to test the upper limits of my capabilities in my athletic pursuits and in my work.

Drive is the vital energy that propels us forward. But while drive pushes an athlete to do everything required to compete at her highest level, I believe that every athlete has her own unique source of motivation. For example, some athletes are clearly driven by money and fame. Other athletes are driven by a deep-rooted need to be the best at whatever it is that they do, while still others simply find that they are happiest when they are training to compete. And some athletes are pushed into a sport at an early age by their parents, who reward them when they do well and punish them when they fall short, planting within them some very deep-seated psychological sources of motivation.

While there are many other sources of drive, I believe that my own drive is rooted in a need to prove myself. As an individual with a disability, I was handed excuses on a silver platter—no one would think less of me if I were not a high achiever. But I am a high achiever, and excuses aren't good enough for me. I needed to prove to myself that I was capable of more than what the world expected of me. As my confidence increased, so did my ambition. Today my drive comes from an excitement about all the things that are possible in my life. I do not believe that I have yet reached my limit; in fact, I'm nowhere close. I have proved that I'm capable of achieving whatever goals I set for myself. What remains now is a voracious appetite to explore the upward trajectory of my abilities to see where it will take me.

THE FUEL, FIRE, BLAZE
GOAL HIERARCHY

The system I developed to achieve the big goals I set for myself is the secret of my success in my athletics, my career, and my life. I have been blessed with the natural gifts that I need to compete— the physical and mental attributes and toughness—but there has to be a vehicle that I can use to transform these natural gifts into success. This vehicle is my goal achievement hierarchy. The good news is that anyone can use this approach to transform his own natural gifts into success. I will show you exactly how to apply the goal achievement hierarchy in your own life.

The question posed to me was, "How do you maintain your drive?" How was I able to maintain the drive to continually push through in spite of exhaustion and all the challenges that life throws at me? I determined that the reason I was able to sustain a heavy workload and always push through was that I was driving toward a goal that meant something to me. In some intrinsic way, I had linked my day-to-day efforts to a higher-level goal that I cared enough about to never give up on. It was on this reflection that I formalized my hierarchy.

The Blind Ambition goal hierarchy has three levels, as shown in Figure 2-1.

Fuel

At the bottom of the figure are what I call *fuel* goals, which provide the foundation for your higher-level goals. Fuel goals are your base goals—the day-to-day tasks you will need to engage in and complete in order to put the rest of the hierarchy in motion so that you can achieve your highest-level goals. Fuel includes anything that

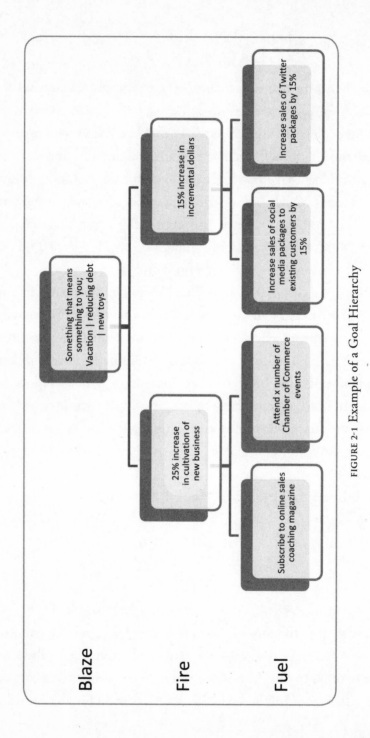

FIGURE 2-1 Example of a Goal Hierarchy

Blaze

Fire

Fuel

Something that means something to you; Vacation | reducing debt | new toys

15% increase in incremental dollars

25% increase in cultivation of new business

Increase sales of Twitter packages by 15%

Increase sales of social media packages to existing customers by 15%

Attend x number of Chamber of Commerce events

Subscribe to online sales coaching magazine

supports your higher-level goals, such as learning about technology, adopting new skills, and recruiting help when necessary.

The key component of a fuel goal is that it must be relevant to your higher-level goals. It must link logically to your blaze goal. If it is not propelling you forward, then it is holding you back. While you are defining your fuel goals, it is a good time to clean up all the efforts you are making that aren't helping you progress. Many activities may appear worthwhile but may not be meaningful in the long term.

Fire

In the middle of the figure are two second-level goals that are the specific milestones necessary for you to achieve blaze—your highest-level goal. I call these second-level goals *fire*. In the figure, the fire goals are "25% increase in cultivation of new business" and "15% increase in incremental dollars." Fire goals are the milestones that are required if you are to make that higher-level goal come true. These are the achievable pillars that you must make happen in order to enable the success of your emotionally motivated blaze goals.

The key component of a fire goal is that it be essential to supporting your blaze goal. It must link to something that you feel strongly about. There must be some hope or internal inspiration. The usefulness of linking your milestones to something that you care about is that it transforms your own motivation to one of accountability. You are now responsible for maintaining your own sense of drive, as you've linked it to something that you stand for, something that you care enough about that it defines you as a person.

Blaze

At the very top of this figure is the highest-level goal, what I call *blaze*, which is the place where your greatest passion intersects with your greatest practice. It's your dream made real. In the example, this goal is "Something that means something to you: vacation/ reducing debt/new toys." The blaze goal is your opportunity to structure your life around something that you sincerely feel strongly about—something that makes you want to jump out of bed in the morning. The blaze goal is the breakthrough moment that you want to facilitate in your life. The key to a blaze goal is that it transcends external validation. All that matters is that you feel strongly about it.

The key component of a blaze goal is not that the goal is ambitious by anyone else's standards; the key is that the goal is important enough to you. It has to come from your heart. Potential energy in a person is mass times gravity times hardship. The force of potential energy that will propel you will come from your heart. Your blaze goal need not be important to anyone other than you. External validation is a moot point. Your heart is the key variable.

One of the traps we all fall into is getting involved in activities that are tangential to our real purpose. For example, if my work goal is to help design and implement a new accounting system for the Chicago sales office, and I spend a couple of days helping a group of coworkers get their office computers moved to a different workspace and back on the office network, then I am not doing the activities that I need to do if I am to achieve my real purpose. As a result, I am putting timely accomplishment of my most important goal at risk.

Linking your activities to your blaze goal can help you identify those activities that aren't helping to move you forward. It is not enough to be busy; you need to be focused on the *right* investments of your time. We all have external commitments. I don't mean to suggest that you cut out all activity that is external—only that you make your commitments and investments of time thoughtful and purposeful. Focused effort is critical—there is only so much time in the day. Focus takes organization and requires making difficult decisions along the way.

Although Figure 2-1 has only two fire goals and four fuel goals supporting the blaze goal, in reality, you can have any number of fire and fuel goals. As you construct your goal hierarchy, just keep in mind that if you set too many goals for yourself, that will make them harder to achieve, which could, in turn, impede you from achieving your blaze goal.

So, where do we start? Establishing a goal achievement hierarchy starts with first identifying one of your highest-level blaze goals. If you are familiar with the work of Jim Collins and Jerry Porras and their book *Built to Last: Successful Habits of Visionary Companies*, these highest-level goals are what they call BHAGs, or Big Hairy Audacious Goals.[3] According to Collins and Porras, a BHAG has the following characteristics: "A true BHAG is clear and compelling, serves as a unifying focal point of effort, and acts as a clear catalyst for team spirit. It has a clear finish line, so the organization can know when it has achieved the goal; people like to shoot for finish lines."

While Collins and Porras's idea of a BHAG may be suitable for organizations, it really doesn't adequately portray the spirit of the top-level blaze goal in my hierarchy. The only real criteria for a blaze goal are that it means something to you as an individual and that it is something that you feel inspired by every day. This could be something like paying for college, earning a promotion, or saving up for a particularly exotic vacation. A blaze goal does not have to be big, hairy, or audacious. It just needs to be important to you on an emotional level.

This goal should be devoid of external validators. In defining your highest-level goal, avoid using language that may mean something to anyone other than you.

I'll never forget the day I accomplished my goal of completing a marathon. My first marathon came only six months after my first half marathon. I was broke, as all college students tend to be, so I headed to the race site in Portland, accompanied by my close friend Cindy Weanling, on an affordable but uncomfortable Greyhound bus. We had nowhere to stay in Portland (and no extra cash to pay for a hotel room), so we slept on a friend of a friend's back porch. We got up at 4:00 a.m. to take public transportation down to the starting line. I can still remember it as clearly as if it happened just yesterday. It was a beautiful day in Portland, sunny with no rain in sight. I was more nervous than I had ever been in my life. The longest I had run in training had been 18 miles, and I was not even sure I would be able to finish the race. I was experiencing tremendous waves of self-doubt, and I began to wonder what people would think of me if I decided to bail. Honestly, I suspected that no one would really care one way or the other. What I did know is that I would never forgive myself for training so hard and not making the attempt.

The heated debate in my head was immediately silenced when the air horn blew and the race began. Without thinking, I started to run, one foot in front of the other. I started out strong, with the 3:35 pace group. As it turned out, this pace proved to be a little too ambitious for me at the time. I lasted about 4 miles before I dropped to a slower pace. I settled into a rhythm and kept a steady pace. My mind wandered as the miles fell away. I felt a deeply emotional appreciation for all my hard work and for my own dedication to creating a better life for myself. I imagined all the indulgent foods I would eat at the finish, and how I would savor their flavors and their smells. I imagined how exciting it would be to rejoin my friend Cindy. I was moved by the fact that she cared enough about me to come to Portland with me and help me toward my goal. I snapped back to the real world when I hit mile 18 and disaster nearly struck.

I had not taken any nutrition during the course of the race, and I was quickly becoming dehydrated in the warm sunshine. My pace slowed tremendously as my body began to shut down. At mile 20, someone handed me a GU, which I had never tried before. In case you're not a distance runner, a GU is an energy gel—a sugar-based frostinglike substance containing electrolytes and sometimes caffeine that your body is able to absorb quickly and use as a fuel source—contained in a small foil packet. Distance athletes rely on them to maintain their blood sugar throughout a race. Fortunately, the GU was exactly what I needed. I gradually pulled myself together and trudged to the finish. Each mile marker brought delight, as I knew that I was that much closer to my goal.

Crossing the finish line was one of the magical moments of my life. I knew with certainty that I was not a person who was going to strive to keep up with my peers. Instead, I was now a person who was going to strive to lead my peers. I had never felt so capable and so able, even when I had full vision. In that moment, I felt that my ability to focus and work hard made up for any disability I had to cope with. There really were no limits to what I could do. And my work had just begun.

My fuel was the commitment to run every day. My fire was the goal of a marathon as a milestone for myself. My blaze was a very deep desire to demonstrate my own self-worth. I consider the successful completion of my first marathon to be one of my greatest accomplishments. I value that race more than any world championship that I have ever won or world record that I have ever set. There were no articles or press releases about my finish. There was no cheering squad to meet me at the end, no group of excited fans to lift me up onto their shoulders. The accomplishment was completely devoid of external validators—I ran the race for me alone and for no one else.

Finishing that first marathon was a statement to myself and to the world that I was taking control of and accountability for my future. Actually, moving a distance of 26.2 miles was a subplot. This was my opportunity to believe that I am a person who starts something and follows through to the end. No matter what anxiety, self-doubt, sadness, or fear I might face along the way, I felt at that moment that I was capable of doing whatever it took to reclaim my future. That vision I had always had of a better self was now within my grasp.

Achieving my goal broke down a wall of disbelief within me. Achieving my goal opened up for me a new world of unlimited opportunities based on the foundation of that first success. I had proved to myself that I was worth something—I had value in this world. I had learned that my own positive transformation was perfectly and precisely within my control, and I made the transition from a state of hopelessness to one of hope.

I kept running.

This initial push launched me on an upward trajectory that cleared the path before me. I now knew that if I set high goals, determined some key milestones, and worked toward those milestones, I could make a meaningful contribution to this world.

When you set a blaze goal, you are making a commitment to success. However, even deeper than that, when you set a blaze goal, you are actually connecting your subconscious reasoning to your conscious reasoning so that they work together to help you achieve exactly what you want to achieve. Think about it for a moment. When you set a goal such as getting a promotion at work or completing a half marathon race, what are the real goals behind the highest-level goal that you have selected?

Consider the example of my inaugural marathon, where my blaze goal was to rebuild my self-worth. It is not hard to stay motivated if you link your milestones and your accomplishments to something that you care passionately about. At the top of your hierarchy may be putting your child through a good university. Link that to the promotions and deliverables that you need to secure over the next several years. Then further link these promotions and deliverables to your day-to-day activities. When you're feeling sluggish or unmotivated, imagine your child in his or her graduation cap and gown. Your emotional self will connect with your analytical self, then watch as you fly through your day-to-day fuel tasks, achieve all your fire milestones, and then succeed in giving your child an opportunity to have a dazzling future.

Take a look at Figure 2-2 for a moment. This figure describes exactly how to use the goal hierarchy to achieve your blaze goals. As in Figure 2-1, your blaze goal is at the very top of the figure. In setting a blaze goal, define a goal that inspires you. Visualize a rocket flying with such tremendous force that it is propelled beyond the earth's atmosphere—a rocket that has exceeded escape velocity.

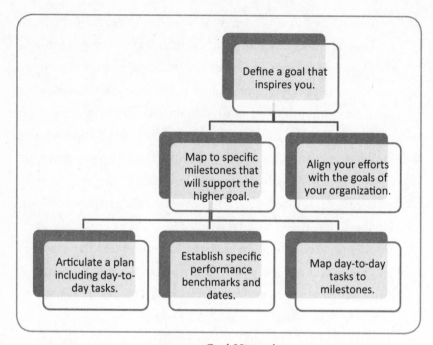

FIGURE 2-2 Goal Hierarchy

Each of us has the ability to make meaningful change, and each of us has the potential energy to change the world as we know it. Your blaze goal is closely linked to your purpose—it is that sense of doing something important that inspires you and moves you forward. For me, this is the sincere hope and desire that no disabled individual who comes after me should have to experience the terrible feeling of being damaged goods. I want to serve as an example of someone with a disability who is not defined by that lack of ability. I want to change my world by changing the perception of athletes with disabilities so that they are taken more seriously.

APPLYING THE FUEL, FIRE, BLAZE GOAL HIERARCHY

1. Define a blaze goal. Identify a goal that is important to you, one that will inspire you and motivate you to leap out of bed every morning with this goal in mind.
2. Determine the fire milestones required to accomplish the blaze goal.
3. Define the day-to-day fuel tasks required to support the fire goals.
4. Define at least one activity that you are doing today that is tangential to the blaze goal—one thing that you could stop doing tomorrow so that you will be able to spend more time on accomplishing your blaze goal.
5. Put together your hierarchy.

PUTTING FUEL, FIRE, BLAZE TO WORK

How exactly do you put the fuel, fire, blaze goal hierarchy to work in setting and achieving your highest-level goals? It all begins with defining a blaze goal. Determine your blaze goal by considering your deepest, most sincere passions. Envision the change that you want to make in your world, or the one thing that you most want to attain in life. Let's assume, for a moment, that your blaze goal is to earn a promotion at work, and the increased responsibilities and pay raise that go along with it.

Once you have figured out what your blaze goal is, then you can take the next step: setting your second-level fire goals. Your fire goals are the milestones you need to achieve to facilitate your forward motion toward the achievement of your blaze goal. To reveal your fire goals, ask yourself, "What steps must I take to support my dream?" Your fire goals must be linked to specific milestones that will support the blaze goal. In the case of a blaze goal of getting a promotion, your fire goals could include improving your measurable work output, taking on a leadership role on a new initiative, or expanding your depth of specialized knowledge.

At the bottom of the hierarchy are the day-to-day tasks—the fuel goals—that you'll need to carry out if you are to accomplish your fire goals. In the case of a promotion at work, these day-to-day tasks could include completing components of important projects, contributing to a trade publication to become recognized as an expert, or taking advanced classes in your field of expertise. Fuel includes anything that can support your higher-level goals. This could include joining a professional association or finding a mentor to offer you guidance. It is the day-to-day efforts that will contribute to your success. Fuel goals are the stepping-stones to accomplishing a higher-level goal.

Setting and actually accomplishing fuel goals—the day-to-day commitments required to achieve the milestones that are linked to your blaze goal—is by far the most challenging step you will take in putting your goal achievement hierarchy in motion. This represents the bulk of the work and requires the greatest discipline and expenditure of power.

The idea that drives the goal hierarchy is to map out your day-to-day routine in such a way that you can achieve what you care deeply about, your blaze goal. So in those moments when you are feeling doubtful, discouraged, or disengaged (and believe me, you'll feel all that and more), you can remind yourself of the real value of the day-to-day tasks that are taking you one step closer to what you really care about.

The other benefit of this approach is that when you are faced with a task that's not in keeping with your long-term vision, you are better able to quickly identify it as a tangential distraction that is not going to help you toward your goal, so that you can eliminate it or avoid it altogether. Doing so will free up more energy for your highest-level goal. Adhering closely to your goal hierarchy will help you to better manage your time, energy, and efforts.

Your blaze goal will become real when you see that big dream that you care so deeply about come true—when your promotion affords you the opportunity to take the family on a vacation, or when you see your child graduate with top honors. All the work, all the fuel, and all the fire will have been worth it.

I started my career at Microsoft as an intern who, in all likelihood, was a long shot for full-time employment. Because of my visual impairment, I had less experience with computers than my coworkers did, and this was a very real problem. Adaptive technology, such as Braille displays and screen readers, is inherently slower and often behind the times, and I was required to absorb visual information in alternative formats. I started at a distinct disadvantage to my peers.

Soon after I started working at Microsoft, I decided to create a blaze goal: to achieve financial security for myself. I was well aware of the challenges I would face in securing a financially solvent future. I had to adopt the attitude that no matter what level of impairment I had, and no matter what my disadvantages were, I would do whatever was necessary to rise to the occasion. I decided that if you took away my screen, or even my keyboard, I would still find a way to succeed. Just leave me the power cord. I do need the power cord.

I had proved to myself that I was capable. My blaze was to transform that capability into financial sovereignty. Financial sovereignty would come through ongoing employment and advancement within the Microsoft hierarchy. In order to secure ongoing employment and advancement, I would have to keep up with, if not exceed, my peers. My challenge was to maintain a comparable workload from a disadvantaged position, while battling misconceptions about blindness. I would have to work longer, harder, and smarter in order to advance. In this pursuit, fuel, fire, blaze became a critical tool for organizing my time and efforts. My blaze was achieving financial security. My fire was to take on some of the bigger features in the Microsoft Outlook e-mail messaging software program. My fuel was the day-to-day activities—accomplished over the course of my 12- to 16-hour workdays—required to overcome any misconceptions and improve my utilization of tools.

The challenge before me was very real. I knew full well that my blaze goal would not be an easy one to achieve. According to the National Federation of the Blind, only 36.8 percent of working-age blind adults are employed, and 31 percent of blind adults live below the poverty line.[4] As a professional in software engineering, I have met only one other blind engineer. While I am not the first by any stretch of the imagination, I am one of the very few blind people who has completed a degree in computer science and electrical engineering and found employment. In order to secure financial sovereignty, I had to overcome all the odds against me.

If you want to advance in your company, you need to be working on something that is meaningful in terms of the organization's objectives. When I first started working at Microsoft, I could clearly see that the opportunities to do this were being reserved for others. So, instead of wishing and hoping that management might eventually decide to give me a try, I took action.

As a software design and test engineer at Microsoft, I was initially given lower-end tasks, that is, working on older features that saw less play. I recognized immediately that this was akin to sitting on the sidelines in physical education class, stacking blocks while the others battled on the court. I knew that in order to prove my competence, I would need to complete the automated testing for these features, cultivate successful relationships with my peers, and ask for more responsibility. I had to demonstrate progress at work by doing everything that was requested of me and then demanding job enlargement.

As I was able to demonstrate an ability to complete the tasks I was given, my higher-ups had increased confidence in my ability to take on higher-level assignments. As I continued proving myself and changing their perception of my abilities, I became less impaired. I was offered an opportunity to take on higher-level, marquee features. For Outlook 2007, there was a transformation in design from the older-style toolbars and menus to a brand-new ribbon designed to help users find the commands they needed to complete a task more quickly. Writing the test automation, updating all existing libraries, and creating new tools for testing this transformation, which touched all components of the mature software program, was a huge leap in responsibility. I fought for the opportunity to be the sole owner of the user interface (UI) feature, as I knew that this would be the best chance I had to advance my career by demonstrating that I could create value that had an impact.

I successfully delivered all testing automation and test harness, assuring that when the new UI was released to production, it would have the highest quality possible. As a result, I was promoted, and I felt that I had satisfied all the requirements of that particular goal. I had advanced by applying my fuel, fire, blaze goal hierarchy.

In this case, my blaze goal was to secure advancement. My fire was to develop software features that could be measured as milestones toward advancement, while proving that I was dependable, that I delivered high quality, and that my visual impairment was a moot point. I could be the most impaired person on the team and still be the highest performer. My fire was securing appropriate mentors who had domain knowledge of the underlying technology and dedicating my free time to cultivating a new skill set.

I networked with everyone I could on the development team— and with my own management team—to get a feel for what would be the marquee features in the next release of Microsoft Office. I asked questions like, "What features are they anticipating printing on the box?" "What features will be demoed in the television commercials?" Once I determined what those key, high-impact features were, I began my campaign to become the sole person responsible for at least one of them. If I were to advance, I needed work that gave me an opportunity to exceed people's expectations.

I also needed to build my skills—a vital part of my fuel. I had to improve my C++ and C# coding skills, demonstrate my ability to work with the test harness, and exemplify my awareness of the depth and breadth of the Outlook toolset. Throughout this period when I was cultivating new skills in order to prove my ability, I was working 12 to 16 hours a day and often on weekends. I felt as if I was in over my head, but I stayed true to the blaze goal. I knew that with focused effort, I could chip away each day at the many issues that were standing in my way. I was inspired by the potential to be financially secure. In the process, I cultivated some great working relationships, developed a newfound confidence in my ability, and created a track record and a reputation as a person who follows through with ambitious goals.

Once I had developed the appropriate network of mentors, understood the underlying technology, cultivated the skill set, and prepared a case showing that a blind person was the right choice for this key feature, I went on to socialize the idea. I scheduled one-on-one meetings with all key decision makers. I talked about it all the time to everyone I encountered at work. I got other people talking about the prospect until the idea started to feel normal to people. Maybe it was true—maybe a vision-impaired person really could excel at what was considered a very visual job.

In order to secure the ribbon UI, which was our most influential feature, I had to make the case that a blind person could be entrusted with visual UI. As you can imagine, this was not an easy case to make. I had to work with other, more senior people on the team to understand the underlying object model and develop a strategy for testing the UI without clicking buttons. I then had to argue that the testing would be improved by relying less on visual UI, as I could ensure improved code coverage that was less reliant on subjective measures. I had to prove that, in fact, a blind person was the *best* person to test the UI.

While I was not included in the decision-making process, once the assignments had been made, I was thrilled to learn that I had been moved from the stale, old features of the previous version of the software to being the sole owner of the new user interface. Through successful delivery of automation scripts, updating of mature libraries to include the new UI, and educating my team members on the new UI and related automation, I was able to deliver all the quality promised and secure my advance to the next level. Fuel, fire, blaze helped me organize my efforts in order to accomplish my blaze goal of overcoming all the odds against me and achieving financial sovereignty and security.

Today, my fuel is the day-to-day relentless workouts, the unceasing nutrition management, and the sacrifice of my social life. My fire is the races that I participate in and the world championships that I win. My blaze will be bringing home gold for my country in 2016. Gold in 2016 hits me at the heart level. I want to make my family and my extended network proud of what I have achieved. Equally important, I want to be a catalyst for a societal incineration of the negative perceptions of people with disabilities. I want to change the perception so that people are not surprised to see me—and others like me—do well.

••• LESSONS •••

- Set goals that are specific and precisely defined.
- Set goals that are difficult to achieve and that challenge you to deliver higher levels of performance.
- When you are working in a group or a team, set goals that are group-centric, that is, goals that maximize the individual contributions of each group or team member.
- To increase the probability that you will achieve your goals, write them down and share them with a coworker, a friend, or a member of your family.
- To further increase the probability that you will achieve your goals, send a weekly progress report to the person to whom you gave a copy of your goals.

CHAPTER 3

DEFINE YOUR LIMITS

· · · · · · · · · · · · · · · ·

THE MOTIVATED PEOPLE WILL TELL
YOU SKY IS THE LIMIT BUT THE
DETERMINED PEOPLE WILL TELL YOU
THAT BEYOND THE SKY THERE IS A SPACE.
REPEL CEASELESSLY YOUR LIMITS.

—Douglas Shumba

After I lost my vision, I had plunged to rock botttom. That plunge had proved to be limitless. I was on track to prove that things can always get worse. Now, armed with a few incremental victories, I felt prepared to prove that a positive upward trajectory is equally limitless. Every day, each of us is inundated with real constraints like the availability of time, increasing demands on our attention, fatigue caused by overload, and the emotional fortitude it takes to adapt to an ever-changing landscape full of unknowns.

We are simultaneously besieged with reminders of our perceived limitations, including critics cutting us down, people assuming the least of us, self-doubt, fear of failure, and a dread of looking a fool.

There are inevitable truths that we can't do anything about, and there are matters of perception that we have control over as soon as we choose to. On many occasions, we can remove our own limiting factors by taking control of the things that we have control over. This requires a leap of faith from time to time and a willingness to reframe a problem. This approach is endlessly powerful once the perceptions are removed and you free yourself to achieve.

THE POWER OF PERCEIVED LIMITATIONS

When we are very young children, we know no limits. We are superkids—we are able to imagine things that our older siblings, parents, and acquaintances can't, and we are ready to leap over any barrier that might try to separate us from our goals. However, as we get older, we begin to see the world from a different perspective, one that is starkly colored by the world around us—and by the perceptions of that world that we carry with us wherever we go.

Consider one research project that clearly shows that young people lose their ability to think in "divergent or nonlinear ways" (which the researchers considered critical to the ability to be creative) as they get older. Dr. George Land and his team followed a group of 1,600 children as they grew up. When this group of kids was between the ages of three and five years old, 98 percent of them were able to think in divergent ways, and only 2 percent could not. However, when they reached an age between eight and ten years old, just 32 percent of the 1,600 children in the study could still think divergently—quite a dramatic drop in creativity. Furthermore, things got worse. When the kids reached an age of between thirteen and fifteen years old, only 10 percent could think divergently, while fully 90 percent could not. Finally, when the test was given to a group of 200,000 twenty-five-year-olds, there was another huge decline in creativity. By the time they reached the age of twenty-five, only 2 percent of the people tested could think divergently, while 98 percent could not.[1]

Yes, you read that right: 2 percent. Sometime between the ages of three to five and twenty-five, the 98 percent who no longer had the ability to think divergently had built themselves tiny little boxes that narrowly defined and constrained their future possibilities, and they had climbed right in, closed the lid, locked it, and thrown away the key—perhaps never to find it again.

This is a long way of saying that *we* create our beliefs about the world around us, and this includes our place within it. So, when someone tells you that you should "know your limits," what exactly does that mean? And who exactly is that cautionary morsel intended for? My personal belief is that you should forget your limits—you should "unknow" your limits. Yes, perceived limitations can protect you from the hurt of failure, but failure is part of life. Trying to protect yourself from the risk of failure serves only to stop you from making an attempt, and what possible good can come from not making an attempt? To not make an attempt is to hope that good things will find you. Prosperity isn't going to seek out someone who is afraid to take a risk. Prosperity finds those who make a bet on themselves by abandoning their limits from time to time.

Truth be told, the limits affecting each of us cover the spectrum from inconsequential ones that we unthinkingly break all the time (for example, with each step we take, we constantly break the constraints that gravity invokes upon us) to those that truly have life-or-death consequences (for example, if you jump out of a car that's speeding along the freeway at 100 miles per hour, chances are that you won't survive). I do not mean to suggest that there are no real limits—there clearly are. Each of us has tangible limits that we have to navigate on a daily basis. However, some of these limits are physical (I can't make a 20-foot high jump, no matter how much I train for it—the current women's world record is just over 6 feet, 10 inches, set in 1987),[2] while others are psychological, derived from our beliefs and experience. These are our perceived limitations.

But here's the trick: perceived limitations can be lifted, diminished, pushed aside, and forgotten with the help of awareness, strategy, and a desire to overcome. This was certainly true for me, and it's a common theme among many people who have achieved truly remarkable goals, whatever those goals may be.

One of my pet peeves is when people say something along the lines of, "I'm not a numbers person," or, "I'm no good at reading financial reports." What that really means is that for any of a number of different reasons, these people haven't made any concerted effort to learn what goes into a financial report, what the different numbers mean, and where they come from. It most definitely does *not* mean that these people don't have a natural aptitude for adding or subtracting. If they devoted enough time to learning the details of financial reporting, I suspect that they would be surprised at just how good their "numbers" skills really are.

You will become good at the behaviors and activities that you practice, and the more you work at them and practice and hone your skills, the better you will get at them. It therefore follows that if you hope to overcome a perceived limitation—that you'll never get ahead at work, or that you'll never find the right mate, or that you'll never have a chance of winning a triathlon—a good place to start is by practicing life without that limitation. Practice what it is like to live free of that limitation. This may mean working harder at first. It may mean being more efficient. It may even mean recruiting friends, family, work colleagues, or even strangers to help. It doesn't matter what it takes. Do whatever you need to do to position yourself to feel capable of the task at hand. Everything else will fall into place.

I often make presentations and motivational speeches to groups where I discuss the power of habits. Habits can be remarkably powerful tools, and depending on the habits that you adopt, they can have profoundly positive or profoundly negative consequences—both for your present and for your future circumstances. If you want to remove the perceived limitations that keep you from achieving your dreams, then the solution is to create habits that support the goal you hope to see come to fruition. For example, if you hope to get a promotion, make a habit of reading articles relating to your industry each day, and then position yourself to see emerging opportunities in your market. A simple habit repeated every day can make you invaluable to your institution. When you combine this habit with a diligent and dependable work ethic, that's a combination that just can't be beat.

Every action you take sets a precedent for future actions. Every action is the start of a new habit—a habit that can take you closer to or farther from your goals, or leave you somewhere in between. So think through your actions before you undertake them. Excuses, rationalizations, and justifications serve only to undermine your potential, and the only person who will ultimately feel the disservice is *you*. Be honest with yourself about the habits that you are creating and your accountability for those behaviors. Remember: when you hear excuses out of your mouth, that is a sure sign that you are undermining your own foundation and no one else's.

College was a challenge for me for a variety of reasons, few of which had anything to do with any physical limitations that I might have had. During my university education, I became acutely aware of the difference between a perceived limitation and a real limitation. The world perceived that when it came to the pursuit of my chosen future, my blindness was a gate that was closed and locked, and many people stepped up to play the role of gatekeeper.

When I tried to take a class in discrete math, for example, I had the great fortune of being assigned to a notoriously difficult professor. This guy would give a final exam that had just 10 questions, with each question being worth 10 percent of your final grade. He would then make the questions multiple choice, so that there was no chance of partial credit. And if that wasn't bad enough, each answer had five different options—he would give the correct answer along with the four most commonly made mistakes. So if you worked out the problem, but you got a wrong answer, in all likelihood the wrong answer would appear as one of the options. This was a play on the power of self-doubt—you would see your answer verified, whether it was right or wrong. This approach forced you to second-guess yourself in circles.

The exam responses were submitted using an anonymous identification number, so the professor had no way of telling how any individual student had done. Right before the final exam, he pulled me into his office to give me what I'm sure he thought was some sage advice. He told me that it would be better for me to take an incomplete in the class, skip the final exam, and then decide on an entirely new career path—something that was less rigorous and more

befitting of someone with my physical challenges. He pushed human-
ities at me. He kept saying to me, "In light of your situation . . ."

I realized that he meant well, but his words stung. So many
times I had heard that my hopes would end up being an exercise
first in futility, and then in failure. People would look at me and
say, "Poor Patricia always has to learn the hard way."

But I have to give my professor credit for one thing: his well-
meaning attempt to shield me from futility and failure pushed me
to my very limits. I could no longer accept other people determining my path in life. It was time for *me* to be the one who decided
what my future course would be, and it was time for *me* to take
responsibility for the outcomes—whatever they might be. I knew in
those moments with my professor that I would rather be a person
who failed gracefully than a person who never made the attempt.

As it turned out, I *did* learn the hard way. I learned the hard
way just how capable I really am. I learned the hard way how little
support I actually needed to stand on my two feet. I learned the
hard way that my limitations are only as powerful as I allow them
to be. I have an inherent disadvantage, but I have a variety of tools
that can minimize the impact of that disability. If my blindness
limits me, it will only be because I made the choice to allow it
to happen. In the meantime, I'm happy to work harder, to find
resources, and to diligently maintain forward motion.

It is here that mental toughness and a willingness to make the
attempt came into my life—it was truly a lifeline for me. But it
wasn't easy. I was physically sick to my stomach with discouragement. Unlike the English Channel swimmer who gave in with just
400 meters to go, however, I saw the situation for what it was. I'd
already done the work—the hard part was over. That exam might
kill me, but I was beyond the point of no return. You don't quit

when you are that close. I knew when I took the exam that this was just another opportunity to fight for my vision of a better self—to hold on and follow through to the end, no matter how bad the situation seemed.

I told my professor that I appreciated his intention of helping me avoid another crushing disappointment, but I was going to ignore his recommendation. I put everything I could into making sure that I was ready for that test. I went to every math learning center session. I went to every study group. I even hired a private math tutor. I had the choice of rent or math help, and I chose math help. I knew that the professor had specifically designed the test to weed out the weaker students—40 percent of us were destined to fail the class. I knew that if I failed the class, I would be able to retake it only once, and then the two class grades would be averaged. If I failed this test and then retook the class, I'd have to get an A the second time, or I was out of the engineering college.

But if that wasn't enough pressure, I also knew that if I failed, I'd be proving all the naysayers right. We all have forces of discouragement that are at work in our lives—the world is full of critics. Each of us faces criticism from a variety of sources. Each of us has to struggle against an inner critic. Overcoming this critic and believing in yourself enough to throw caution to the winds and make an attempt anyway is a universal challenge. When you are fighting the critics—internal and external—it is sometimes enough for you just to show up. But sometimes you have to show up ready for the fight of your life. And this was shaping up to be one of those times for me—not life and death in a physical sense, but definitely in terms of my self-esteem and the future that I hoped to achieve.

After I took the test, I suspected that I was going to be in the 40 percent of students who failed. But I was ready for any outcome.

Either I was going to succeed or I was going to fail, and if failure was going to be my destiny, then I would have an opportunity to fail gracefully.

After the dust settled and the anonymous IDs were revealed, I learned that I had not failed after all—in fact, I had earned the third-highest grade in the class. And I learned a valuable lesson about myself—a lesson that I carry with me to this day. If you work hard enough, if you have exhausted all the tools available to help yourself, and if you have prepared yourself to lose everything, then you can and will succeed, no matter what obstacles might be in your way.

Earning the third-highest grade on the math exam taught me that perceived limitations are different from real limitations, and that I had the power to break down any of my perceived limitations. The same is true for you. You have perceived limitations—that you're no good at math, or that you're not smart enough to get a promotion, or that you're not the kind of person who is good at presenting in front of a large group of business associates—and you have real limitations like time, money, and demands for your attention. And when it comes to your limitations, whether perceived or real, there will always be naysayers who are ready to tell you what you can't do and what dreams you should just forget about.

Here's *my* advice: be polite and be graciously thankful for the advice of family members, friends, professors, and work colleagues, but rely on your own judgment at the end of the day. No matter how well meaning the advice that you receive from these people might be, it's your life, and you are the one who knows best what you can and cannot accomplish. Not only that, but you are the one who will have to live with the results of this advice, whether good or bad. I love my friends and family and often seek their council; however, I am accountable for the final decision.

People have all sorts of excuses for failure—they set themselves up for it. I will listen to their reasons and then ask myself, "Are they trying to convince *me* or themselves?" More often than not, they are trying to convince themselves of some limitation that is perceived and not real. The good news on this front is that we have control over our perception. Those things that you see as limiting you today can dissipate with concerted effort and deliberate thinking. Use every tool in the toolbox to help yourself, seek help from others when necessary, and make a bet on yourself, and you will see those perceived limitations fade over time.

For me, an example of a real limitation would be those very rare occupations that really do demand vision. Given the technology that currently exists, becoming a brain surgeon is not a viable career path for me. That is not a perception—that is a reality. But there is nothing standing in the way of my being a successful engineer. Would it be easier with vision? Sure, that is inarguable. That being said, I am still a productive, contributing engineer using technology and focused energy to set myself apart. I find new and innovative ways to bring unique leadership to my every occupation.

My understanding of perceived versus real limitations helped me complete my degree in electrical engineering and computer science at Oregon State University and complete my masters in executive nonprofit leadership at Seattle University—all while working full-time at Microsoft and training full-time for IRONMAN. I have pushed my limits and been pleasantly surprised with the results more often than not.

When you think you have reached your limits, push just a little more. I think you may be surprised to find that you will work harder, achieve more, and accomplish things that you never dreamed possible, if you just believe in yourself and break down the perceived limitations that are holding you back. In fact, I would be willing to bet on it. Give it a try, and see what happens.

DEFINING YOUR LIMITS ON THE JOB

While I was at Microsoft, I was awarded the company's Gold Star, an award that was given to high performers in the company. I earned the award by finding situations where click tracking for online ads was not working properly, resulting in a loss in revenue. By making the correction, I closed the loop on $40,000 per month of revenue that was being lost. But despite the pride I felt in earning the award and recovering almost half a million dollars in annual revenue for Microsoft, one of my work colleagues was very vocal to the effect that he thought I had received the award because of my blindness—that it was a feel-good charity award. His proof was that he was certain that my effort was not actually engineering. To win that award, however, I had to write edits to the code in order to fix it—something that was clearly software engineering. I have learned that no matter what I accomplish, people will think what they are going to think, and there is nothing I can do to change their minds.

Your perceived and real limitations are for you to understand, and no one else. You need to realize that no matter what you do or accomplish, there will still be people running behind you who are trying to belittle your efforts, and people who are trying to claim that you are somehow less than you project. At the end of the day, you have to hold firm in the confidence of what you know to be true. Naysayers are loud, but I have learned that there is no correlation between volume and accuracy.

Henry Ford was known to say, "Whether you think you can or you think you can't, you are usually right." While we all recognize that we do have limitations, both perceived and tangible, we do not always acknowledge our power over our perceived limitations. Overcoming perceived limitations requires a belief in the possibility, dedication to a consistent high-quality effort over time, and the development of a structure and strategy around the goals set.

For many years, people believed that it was not physically possible for anyone to run a mile in less than four minutes. However, in 1954, Englishman Roger Bannister broke the four-minute-mile barrier. Shortly after Bannister broke this barrier, several other runners were able to follow suit. There are two potential explanations for this phenomenon. The first is that Bannister destroyed the perceived limitations that other runners had within them. The second is that several runners believed that this was possible, but because of his training and racing schedule, Bannister was first to the punch. What I glean from Bannister's work is that while belief is a key component, belief in the potential must go hand in hand with diligence, hard work, structure, and strategy. A belief in the possibility complemented by the linking of intrinsic motivation to a meaningful goal can empower you to prove that there is no upper limit to your capabilities.

A personal hero of mine, and a man who exemplifies redefining limits in business, is Elon Musk, an investor and inventor who is responsible for cofounding such endeavors as SpaceX, PayPal, Tesla Motors, and more. Musk was influential in introducing online newspapers, online business directories, high-prestige electric cars, online payments, and now the potential to explore Mars in the future. Imagine a world without online payments or online directories. One person had the power and influence to reinvent the way the world operates by having a willingness to see the world as what he wanted it to be, rather than being limited by acceptance of the status quo. Musk is a genius innovator by any standard, and there is no doubt in my mind that his efforts will continue to change our day-to-day life as we know it.

Imagine what you could do if you also chose to question the limitations that impede your upward trajectory. The question you need to consider is: What is the cost of the propellant? The propellant you'll use to break down your own limitations is your fuel, fire, and blaze. The associated costs are your focused consistent efforts over time toward meaningful goals.

When I am feeling the weight of my own limitations, I think of how Elon Musk has reinvented Internet technology and reusable energy, and his attempt to turn the government monopoly on space exploration into a profit-making enterprise. Both Elon Musk and Roger Bannister overcame their perceived limitations, first through a firm belief in the possibility of being a leader, second through a consistent high-quality effort over time, and third through a structure and strategy for linking day-to-day goals to intrinsically meaningful objectives. Their execution on these goals proves to me that each of us is capable of having a meaningful impact by overcoming our own perceived limitations.

Musk and Bannister both proved that if you dream it, believe it, and dare to attempt it, the impossible may be possible.

Reflect for a moment on your own goals. Ask yourself the following: "What would I do if I had no constraints? What is my dream? What would I dare to do if I were not bound by my training?" Once you have reflected on your own perceived limitations and your own training, determine your highest-level dream. Now, what is keeping you from achieving it? What daring course of action can you take immediately to demonstrate your belief in yourself? What can you do to challenge those perceived limitations?

Consider the case of starting a small business. According to the U.S. Small Business Administration, one-third of new small businesses fail within the first two years, and by year five, approximately half have failed.[3]

The men and women who founded these businesses faced very real limitations. Their products or services were not competitive in the marketplace, or they didn't have sufficient financial resources to keep their businesses afloat long enough, or they may have had a great product, but they didn't know how to manage their people or their business. However, while these limitations may have seemed quite real to the entrepreneurs who experienced them, I personally believe that in many cases, these limitations are perceived ones. Products can be made more competitive; sufficient financing can be secured; people can learn how to manage their people and their businesses more effectively. In each case, the limitations can be overcome. It may not be easy, but it can be done.

Test your limitations—you will impress yourself with how far you can move past your original expectations. Be accountable for the habits that you create. Be purposeful and specific. Every action that you take sets a precedent for the next action. You can move into a downward spiral or into an upward trajectory. The choice is yours, and the direction you ultimately take will be the result of a long series of decisions that you make along the way. Think through your actions and ask yourself whether you intend to create a good habit or a bad habit. Whatever habits you decide to create, choose the ones that lift you up.

Breaking Through the Limits at ViewPlus

Imagine trying to teach physics or math without ever drawing a picture. Imagine trying to describe complex differential equations using auditory information alone. Imagine a classroom with no chalkboard or whiteboard. This was the situation that blind students were in prior to the inventive spirit of Dr. John Gardner. As he lost his vision, Gardner became aware of the abysmal state of STEM (science, technology, engineering, and mathematics) access for blind and low-vision students. He recognized that the technology that existed at that time (the late 1990s and early 2000s) was not sufficient to provide the access that these students required.

Gardner had a choice: to accept the tangible limit as it existed, or to completely turn the system on its head. He chose to change the world for blind students by redefining the limit. He had the physics background, he understood how to get research funded, and he knew the right team of people to engage, including an eager young student by the name of Patricia Walsh—yours truly.

While Braille printers had already been around for some time, they were limited to printing text—graphics such as those required in math and physics were out of the question. We were suggesting the groundbreaking premise that it would be possible to print graphics as well as text. Furthermore, the printers that existed at the time required specialized and expensive proprietary software, and extensive training was needed in order to produce documents. Dr. Gardner's vision was for people to be able to use software that they already owned and knew how to use, such as Microsoft Word, to prepare and print documents without any additional training. Indeed, with every iteration, we brought a product closer to commercial viability.

When I started working for Gardner, the tactile printers were still in preproduction. There was just one machine that was capable of doing line drawings. My initial responsibilities were to proofread the Braille output and provide feedback on the readability of the documents produced. As my technical skill set developed, I grew with the company to take on more advanced roles and responsibilities. We iterated on the design, taking into consideration the sound of printing, the materials printed on, preparation of documents, readability of documents, the styles of Braille printed, and, of course, the availability of graphics.

We launched a grassroots marketing campaign, hitting up all the major conferences to demonstrate what was possible. The original cost of the printer was $10,000, so it was not intended for household use. However, once we got a foothold in a few universities, particularly the Texas State School for the Blind and Visually Impaired (TSSBVI), we could demonstrate a proof of concept that our tool was usable, ready to change lives, and sellable. This enabled us to gain the funding we needed to launch ViewPlus Technologies, a for-profit company. At the age of 19, I was the company's fourth employee. My job was to manage all of our presentations and communications with libraries and universities. The product sold itself. Research continued until we were able to develop a consumer product at a fraction of the cost for Braille printing at home.

Dr. Gardner engaged the right team of hardware engineers, electrical engineers, software engineers, and those who knew Braille (like myself) to accomplish his goals. He also placed a few printers at the most influential institutions for educating the blind, such as TSSBVI. The development process required a great deal of trial and error, but we took the feedback we received and iterated until we had a viable commercial product. We worked tirelessly in order to complete whatever task was at hand. It was a typical start-up mentality where everyone responded to the challenge: we all prepped materials, gave presentations, met with prospective investors, and participated in technical discussions.

Ultimately, we succeeded in creating a Braille printer that could handle graphics just as effectively as it handled text. I was blessed to have participated, and I learned from Dr. Gardner's example. He taught me that there are no limits beyond those that you define for yourself. When Dr. Gardner invited me to join his team, I was studying elementary education during the day and working the graveyard shift at a diner. I didn't realize that becoming an engineer could even be a possibility for me, but it was—and my life changed forever.

People like John Gardner, Elon Musk, and Roger Bannister don't see obstacles—they see opportunities. Instead of allowing limits to define or constrain them, they find ways to get around, over, under, or through those limits, working tremendously hard and smart until they reach the goals they have set for themselves. John Gardner invented a new kind of printer that allowed people with severe vision impairments to "see" graphics for the first time. Elon Musk is redefining the future of space travel and the automobile industry. And Roger Bannister broke the four-minute mile. Think about the limits in your own life, and consider what you can do to shatter them. We all have the ability to achieve great things in our lives—what will you do today to get you closer to *your* goals?

• • • LESSONS • • •

- Make no excuses. Set goals that you are willing to achieve, and do what it takes to achieve them.

- Be polite and be graciously thankful for the advice of family members, friends, professors, and work colleagues, but rely on your own judgment at the end of the day.
- Make a habit of "unknowing" your limits; that is, identify the perceived limitations that you place on yourself and then either ignore them or abandon them altogether.
- For limitations that are more difficult to break through, study what you need to learn, practice your skills repeatedly until they are honed, and work especially hard for however long it takes.
- Constantly test your limitations—you may surprise yourself by finding that what you thought were limits really aren't.

CHAPTER 4

BE AN IRON MAN OR IRON WOMAN

· · · · · · · · · · · · · · ·

THE GREATEST ACCOMPLISHMENT
IS NOT IN NEVER FALLING, BUT IN
RISING AGAIN AFTER YOU FALL.

—Vince Lombardi

One day over coffee, a close friend asked me a question that changed my life: "Have you ever considered doing an IRONMAN?" I hadn't because I didn't know what an IRONMAN was. I had never really known any triathletes, and I wasn't even exactly sure what a triathlon was. However, I tend to go into things head first. I went home that day and signed up for an IRONMAN without even researching the distances. At this point in time, I was a decent runner, I had one bike ride under my belt (to and from several bars), and I wasn't sure whether I did or did not know how to swim. I quickly learned that in fact, I had no idea how to swim. My swim stroke was described kindly by a lifeguard as "hard to watch." It became clear pretty quickly that my years out of the pool, combined with having never had formal swimming lessons, had left me with an inability to swim.

Regardless, I was all in.

THE PSYCHOLOGY OF MENTAL TOUGHNESS

Whether the goals you're setting are personal or business in nature, when they are the kind of blaze goals that are at the highest level and most important to you, it takes a certain amount of mental toughness, persistence, and perseverance over a sustained period of time to achieve them. You can't just be in it for the moment—you have to have a long-term commitment to achieving your goals, no matter how challenging they may be. Not only that, but you must be resilient—that is, you must be able to bounce back when you fail, or when you encounter adversity.

Angela Duckworth is a researcher at the University of Pennsylvania who has devoted more than a decade to the study of how people achieve the goals they set for themselves. According to Duckworth, two traits predict success in life: grit and self-control. Duckworth defines *grit* as "the tendency to sustain interest in and effort toward very long-term goals," while *self-control* is "the voluntary regulation of behavioral, emotional, and attentional impulses."[1] Both of these traits are necessary and complementary ingredients and predictors of success in life. Self-control helps you win the fight against the momentary temptations—the urge to check your smartphone when you hear the chime that accompanies a new text message, or eating a sugary snack that you know you shouldn't—that can derail you from achieving your goals. Grit, on the other hand, helps you keep your eye on achieving your long-term goals over a period of weeks, months, and sometimes even years.

In her TED talk, Duckworth said that grit "is sticking with your future, day in, day out, not just for the week, not just for the month, but for years, and working really hard to make that future a reality. Grit is living life like it's a marathon, not a sprint."[2] In other words, if your blaze goal is to one day become the director of sales for your organization, and you are a new salesperson with just six months of experience under your belt, then you will need to stick with your future goal in some small way each and every workday until you eventually achieve it. It may take you years to make the climb from salesperson to director of sales, but if you have the grit that is necessary to lead you to your blaze goal, then you will certainly achieve it.

To determine the extent of someone's grit, Duckworth and her research team at the University of Pennsylvania have developed several different assessments. The questions in these assessments determine whether or not someone has the personality traits that are indicators of grit, including:

- Whether or not respondents are hard workers
- Whether or not they are discouraged by or have overcome setbacks
- Whether or not previous projects have been routinely left undone because of the distraction of new projects
- Whether or not respondents finish the pursuits that they begin
- Whether or not they have achieved a long-term goal

Angela Duckworth credits Stanford University psychology professor Carol Dweck as inspiring her work on the concepts of grit and self-control, specifically Dweck's research in the area of what she terms the "growth mindset." According to Dweck, people who have a *growth mindset*—that is, people who believe that their most basic abilities can be developed through dedication and hard work—are better able to achieve their goals than those who have a *fixed mindset*, in which they believe that their talent, intelligence, and other traits are fixed and can't be further developed.

People who have a fixed mindset, and who believe that talent, intelligence, and other such traits are static, often plateau early, fail to accomplish their long-term goals, and achieve less than their full potential. They tend to:

- Avoid challenges.
- Give up easily.
- See effort as fruitless . . . or worse.
- Ignore useful negative feedback.
- Feel threatened by the success of others.

On the other hand, people who have a growth mindset believe that talent, intelligence, and other such traits can be developed in themselves, that their brain is like a muscle that can be strengthened, and that they control their own destinies. As a result, they tend to:

- Embrace challenges.
- Persist in the face of setbacks.
- See effort as the path to mastery.
- Learn from criticism.
- Find lessons and inspiration in the success of others.[3]

When you set your own blaze goals and then work to achieve them, step back for a moment and think about your own personal beliefs and attitudes. Do you have the grit you need in order to persevere over the long run, or are you constantly being thrown off track because your self-control needs shoring up? Do you realize that you can grow and achieve more, or are you stuck in the erroneous belief that you are who you are, and you can never break out of that box?

So, how can you improve your own grit while developing the growth mindset that will get you on the road to achieving your long-term blaze goals? In a Forbes.com column, Margaret Perlis pointed to five areas of focus for improvement:

- *Courage.* Don't allow a fear of failure or a fear of looking like you're not smart keep you from taking risks or lead you to avoid challenges. Says Perlis, "Courage helps fuel grit; the two are symbiotic, feeding into and off of each other . . . and you need to manage each and how they are functioning together."
- *Conscientiousness.* Of the Big Five core character traits that psychologists believe all human personality types possess, conscientiousness is the one that is most closely related to grit. However, it can't be just any kind of conscientiousness; it has to be the kind that has you stepping out of your baseline routines. According to Perlis, "It is important to commit to go for the gold rather than just show up for practice."
- *Follow-through.* Make long-term commitments and work hard to follow through on them. Don't allow yourself to get off track or to let short-term distractions or day-to-day obstacles get in your way.

- *Resilience.* Understand that failure is just a short stop on the way to achieving your goals, whatever they may be. Be optimistic, be confident in your own abilities (but be willing to learn and improve), and be creative and constantly seek new routes to achieving your goals when the ones you tried don't get you where you want to go.
- *Excellence versus perfection.* Realize that you don't need to be perfect, or, in the words of a currently popular truism, "Expect perfection, but accept excellence." As humans, we will never be perfect—at least not for very long. However, we can routinely be excellent, and by living with an attitude of excellence, we can achieve even our most challenging goals.[4]

Setting and Achieving My IRONMAN Goals

An IRONMAN triathlon competition is like no other. First there's a 2.4-mile swim, immediately followed by a 112-mile bike race, and ending with a 26.2-mile, full marathon-length run. Any one of those events alone is enough to wear out most athletes. But when you put them all together, one right after another, you've got a recipe for an event that is truly the ultimate test of human physical and mental endurance.

I signed up for swimming lessons and started researching how to get a guide for the tandem. I was by far the slowest in the pool, and I panicked when I put my head in the water. My answer to that was just to never put my face in the water. (For those who don't swim, having your head out of the water is like trying to drive with the emergency brake on, or like pressing the gas and the brake at the same point. You won't get very far, and if you do, it won't be pretty.) The water was very disorienting to me. I couldn't hear well, and I couldn't see at all. I felt complete sensory deprivation in the water, and I struggled as I tried to swim from one side of the pool to the other.

I wanted to test whether I could even complete a 2.4-mile swim. So I did the math—I converted miles to yards, then yards to lengths, and figured out how many laps it would take to complete a 2.4-mile swim in a pool. It should be obvious by now that I had no coach, and my better judgment was still pretty bad. So I swam my first IRONMAN distance swim after about two weeks of lessons in a local community pool. It took three hours. I was exhausted—I felt as if I had just run 10 marathons back to back. I had to call a friend to come pick me up at the gym, since I was too tired to walk home. My friend said that he was on the way to a barbecue. He could give me a ride home later, but for now I had to go with him.

By a remarkable coincidence, at the barbecue I met someone who had gone to college with Aaron Scheidies, the world's fastest blind male triathlete. It just so happened that he lived only half a mile from me. I never saw that friend of a friend again, but he helped me connect with Aaron, and my life changed. Aaron was dialed into blind athletes. Magazines and sponsors took Aaron seriously. Aaron was doing something that I had never considered possible. I was participating, but Aaron was competing. I wanted to compete.

My first IRONMAN race was at Lake Placid, the second-oldest IRONMAN competition in North America. The setting is idyllic, beginning with a swim in Mirror Lake, a bike ride through the Adirondack Mountains, and a marathon run through the countryside around the town of Lake Placid, New York. The goal I set for my first IRONMAN was just to finish the race—that in itself would be a huge accomplishment, and it was the center of my focus for many months as I trained for the race.

I started the race frantic because I had forgotten my tether. A swimmer near us "MacGyvered" a swim tether for us on the spot by splitting a bike inner tube in half. It was one of the best tethers we had ever used. We finished our 2.4-mile swim under the cutoff, but just barely. We got on the tandem. The course was more hill than flat, and the miles went on and on. The headwinds were brutal, but the downhills were our saving grace. We got that tandem flying at 45 to 50 mph—completely out of control. It is a miracle that we didn't crash, but we needed those downhills to make up for how hard it is to push a tandem up a hill. Finally, we had survived the worst, and we made it to the run. Thank God the run was last, as that is my only strength in this sport.

I finished the IRONMAN Lake Placid, which was exactly what I had set out to do. I didn't break any records, but that hadn't been my goal. My goal had been to finish the race, and I had. My time was a respectable 14 hours 38 minutes. However, this turned out not to be my last IRONMAN, and I would improve that time considerably.

Six weeks after completing IRONMAN Lake Placid, I received a phone call while I was lying in bed with a bag of potato chips, watching the same reruns of *30 Rock* that I'd seen a hundred times before. A professional athlete called to ask if I wanted to race an IRONMAN with her in the coming year. "Yes!" I shouted into the receiver of the phone. I threw out the chips, turned off the TV, sprinted to the gym, and started training immediately. That day I did a four-hour, high-intensity bike ride.

Now that I had a chance to race with my hero, I was committed to putting my entire heart and soul into being as fast as possible.

I determined that since I had finished IRONMAN Lake Placid in
14:38, then 13:00 was an ambitious, but achievable goal. But I had
read an article that said that people are far more likely to deliver
on a goal if they commit to it publicly. So, while my personal
goal was 13:00, I told everyone I knew that my goal was actually
12:00. Coming in anywhere near 13:00 would be a miracle, but I
committed to 12:00 just to add an extra push.

Aaron set up a training program for me, focusing on swimming and cycling. We started immediately. I have never worked so
hard in my life. I was reliably at the gym by 5:15 a.m. every day,
then off to work for a 10-hour day in the office, then back to the
gym, then home to work on my graduate school homework. I was
averaging just three or four hours of sleep a night. But I wasn't
complaining—I felt that this opportunity had landed in my lap
from the heavens, a once-in-a-lifetime chance to do something
great. I wanted to break every record I knew of, to be in the top
ranks of elite women triathletes.

Time flew by, and soon it was April—just weeks away from the
competition. It was time to finalize last-minute details, such as
flights, meals, and all the rest. It was then that I got the bad news.
Three weeks before I was supposed to compete in IRONMAN Texas,
my guide, my hero, had to exit gracefully. She had a sponsorship
issue that she had not anticipated, and I was left out in the cold.
But I didn't cry about it, nor did I shake my fist in frustration. I
just resigned myself to the fact that from time to time, these wild
ambitions don't pan out the way you expected. And I decided that
one way or another, I would ensure that my dream didn't die a
premature death.

Consider for a moment that there are very few athletes in the
world who can do a 13-hour IRONMAN and virtually none who

can do a 13-hour IRONMAN with just three weeks' notice—and that the very few who could possibly do it are probably training for their own race. So I knew that my chances of finding a fill-in guide three weeks before the race were next to none. It is exactly during moments like this that I find myself remembering the story of the woman swimming the English Channel. I could see that I was only 400 yards from making history. No one would think less of me for quitting, as I had a valid excuse. But I knew that I would never live it down if I didn't push to the very end.

So I exhausted *every* possibility. I contacted other professionals. I tapped into networks of athletes. I called news stations. I talked to priests. I stopped homeless people who I thought could potentially possess some magical enchantment. I grasped at any shard of hope I could hang onto. I was in a frenzy.

Then, the good news that I had hoped for came. With the help of Matt Miller, founder of the C Different Foundation, I did not find just one guide, I found two. By some miracle, Matt knew two of the most elite amateur female athletes in the country, and both women—Sonja Week and Michelle Ford—happened to be training for the IRONMAN Kona competition, scheduled for October. They were in the best shape of their lives, and they needed to train in hot weather, while I desperately needed a guide for a race in hot weather. Michelle agreed to guide me on the swim and bike portions of the race, and Sonja agreed to guide me on the run.

Thursday we went through registration and took care of a few logistical loose ends. Friday was our only chance to train together. Michelle and I did a 400-yard swim to acquaint us with guiding in the water. We managed to navigate a giant floating cone with ease. This was all the practice we were going to get before our 2.4-mile swim the next day. After the brief swim, Michelle and I hit the bike for a practice round. We rode a 200-yard practice loop around the parking lot to prepare ourselves. It wasn't much, but it was better than nothing.

The swim is and always will be the hardest portion of a triathlon for me. I can't see light in the water, and I cannot hear. It's nearly complete sensory deprivation for me. In the water, communication with my guide is restricted to just two things: being punched to go right, or tugged on a tether to go left. Add 2,000 other swimmers in a confined space, and you have a surefire recipe for panic. Fortunately, I have learned half a dozen meditations to keep my brain calm, and I am now able to keep this strange sensation of my brain pulsing with anxiety mostly under control.

It turned out to be the most seamless swim I have ever completed. Our communication in the water was perfect—it was as if we had been teamed together for years. I did swim over Michelle a few times, causing us both to lose momentum, but we both regained speed quickly. We navigated a tight course, even passing a few people, and we finished the swim with a respectable time of 90 minutes. We sprinted from the water to the bike.

The moment we left the water, my entire fiber changed. I was now in my element, and I felt strong and in control. As soon as we clipped into the bike and started on our 112-mile bike ride, the thought passed through my mind that I was feeling mean as hell. I remember being shocked at this revelation. But I was overflowing with a passion for one thing: to *destroy* this race. I cycled faster than I ever had before in any training ride, faster than I knew was possible. Michelle was an amazing guide. We were smooth as butter. We hit gravel once, but even then we maintained our cool and our rocket-fast pace. We were having the time of our lives while we were destroying this course.

We completed the bike course, and it was time to make the transition to the last segment of the IRONMAN: the run.

We jumped off the bike, sprinted into the transition tent, and met up with Sonja. I madly switched shoes, and then Sonja and I headed back out of the tent to start the marathon. We were at 7 hours. This meant that achieving my personal goal of 13 hours would require a 6-hour marathon. However, achieving my publicly stated goal of 12 hours meant running a 5-hour marathon. The one discipline in IRONMAN that I feel I am really strong at is the run. I was astonished that a 12-hour IRONMAN was within my grasp—I was inspired and deeply motivated.

By the time the marathon rolled around, the temperature was 95 degrees, and at mile 3 of the run, my intestines gave out. So we stopped at every porta-potty on the route, which slowed us down. We had started at 7-minute miles, but with my GI issues, we were now up to 10-minute miles. We were still on track for our marathon, but just barely. Fortunately, I got progressively faster with every mile. Our goal was now on target handily. From 10-minute miles, we moved down to a 9-minute mile, then down to 8:40, then 7:40, and finally held steady at 7.

As we were running, I noticed that people were cheering really loudly at different spots along the course. For miles, I wondered what in the world had gotten them so excited. We were moving at a serious clip by this point. Sonja was occupied yelling, "Blind runner!" as we passed people left and right. One man fell to the ground in tears at the prospect of being passed by a blind woman.

We kept moving along, embraced by the heat and passing with a vengeance. Finally, at mile 21 of the marathon, and in the spirit of the moment, I threw my arm up—a gesture of excitement for the sport and for the race. The crowd exploded. I had heard them cheering loudly as we passed, but it hadn't occurred to me that they were cheering for me. The eruption of cheers and applause surged through my backbone. Every millimeter of my nervous system was on fire. We dropped from a 7-minute mile to a 6:50, and then from a 6:50 to a 6:40, which we maintained through to the finish. I couldn't believe it.

I realized that we were making history, and I began to acknowledge to myself that the dream that I had fought so hard to make real was coming true. With every step, we were that much closer to a world record. We met Michelle on the course with 200 yards to go, and we crossed the finish line as a team. When we crossed the line, the volume of the crowd multiplied many times, and I knew it was for us.

I knew we had the record, but I didn't know what our time was.

I turned to Sonja and Michelle, yelling over the crowd, "What did we do?!? What did we do?!?" Sonja told me that we had hit the finish line at exactly 11:40, shattering my personal goal of 13 hours and comfortably achieving my public goal of 12 hours. I am not one for tearing up, and I didn't at that moment, but I sure did later when we had a minute alone. At that instant, I soaked in every sound, smell, and feeling that I could. I was at the crest of a personal dream come true.

Looking back, I know how it felt to be the woman who swam the Channel in my childhood story. I almost gave up before I started. My 400 yards to go was the starting line. I had powered through the fog. I had powered through the terror, the exhaustion, and the doubt. I had risked failure to achieve my goal. My dreams had come true, but I knew it was no accident.

I broke the world record for blind and low-vision athletes, and I came in thirteenth out of 600 competitors in my age group. With the help of Sonja and Michelle, IRONMAN Texas was all I needed to launch my business, Blind Ambition. I saw that all the strength and confidence that I had built up had positioned me naturally to help others achieve their highest aspirations. I have no genetic gift or ability, and I have no special talent to speak of. What I do have is organization, drive, and consistency. And I have a unique and tested approach to goal setting—an approach that is at the heart of the chapters that follow.

BEING AN IRON MAN OR IRON WOMAN AT WORK

Think for a moment about your own accomplishments. Do you feel that you have an innate ability that is fixed and doesn't change, or do you feel that you have been propelled forward as a direct result of the skills you have cultivated over time? I honestly know of no one in any industry who has excelled as a result of luck alone. The studies researching the impact of talent versus training and education are seemingly limitless. The logic becomes circular—is a person good at what she does because she is talented, or is she good because she enjoys what she is doing and has put in the extra hours?

My personal experience in both athletics and business leads me to lean in the direction of practice makes perfect. I did not have any particular privilege in my upbringing, and I was not fostered to demonstrate talent. My ability to be successful has come from having a capacity for adaptability, that is, the growth mindset that psychologist Carol Dweck believes is the key to success.

As an engineer at Microsoft, it was critical that I learn the C++ and C# computer programming languages, and doing so was instrumental to my ability to take on the projects that fueled my career growth at the company. As I have since moved on from this position, new skill sets have become key. For example, I now need to have the ability to create technical documents and statements of work for international joint ventures, including the technical detail required to solidify the commitments that have been made. This has required me to adapt and learn an entirely new set of technical skills that will enable me to progress in this new career.

Excelling at just one or two skills is not enough. You need to be able to cultivate the right skills for the task at hand. The world we live in is so remarkably fast-paced that our skill sets may become outdated before our very eyes. The solution is to constantly be open to learning the things that we need to know if we are to stay current in our jobs, while preparing for the next challenge. And throughout it all, we must be iron men and iron women; that is, we must cultivate the grit and the self-control that are required if we are to achieve our most important blaze goals.

As an advisor to the head of engineering at Mozido, my role was to provide end-to-end planning to ensure the success of our many joint ventures around the world. As a start-up company, we were under pressure to be the first to market in offering financial services via mobile phones, smartphones, and feature phones in developing nations. This meant that my objectives changed dramatically from day to day. If I was to succeed, I needed to be able to research and solve problems in near-real time, as events demanded it. One project, for example, required a comprehensive gap analysis of existing financial services in Sri Lanka, including remote check deposit, remittance payments, government services, credit card processing, and on and on. I was responsible for quickly:

- Understanding the population and its needs
- Understanding the existing financial infrastructure, the issues surrounding and the impact of corruption, legislation concerning financial services, regulatory compliance (both national and international), and technology centers
- Figuring out where the gaps in service were from the population and the existing snapshot of financial services

To get ahead of financial services over such a breadth of offerings is no small feat. However, I was able to succeed by mapping the project into the fuel, fire, blaze goal-setting framework. For Sri Lanka, the blaze—the highest-level goal—was to bring trusted financial services via smart and feature mobile phones to people who need those services. Accomplishing the blaze goal required setting fire goals that included developing a trusted service that would ensure the security and reliability of all banking services, including payments, checks, electronic payments, payroll, and more. For the unbanked—those who are new to the idea of putting their money into a bank—this includes educating them on financial services like checking and savings accounts, transforming a cash economy into a banked economy, and cultivating the adoption of mobile access to banking services. The fuel for this task is delivering on this technology, that is, the ongoing planning, execution, and testing of solutions in order to be a global influencer of the adoption of technology. This requires training, educating, acquiring joint venture contracts, and delivering on objectives in order to see the fire and blaze goals to fruition.

I have no innate ability that makes me able to deliver on the recommendations or the research, but what I do have is an iron man/iron woman mentality that keeps me open to learning new knowledge and skills while focusing my effort on the blaze goal of bringing trusted financial services via smart and feature mobile phones to people who need such services. And I have the experience and a track record of being able to solve problems creatively.

My own drive to achieve this blaze goal, as well as a personal dedication to being a lifelong learner, makes it possible for me to stay driven toward discovering new market opportunities for my employer as we grow and develop in an international ecosystem of mobile and financial services. I know that no matter how much knowledge and how much experience I have, I still have a great deal to learn—techniques that will make me more efficient and effective, better applications, a new approach to developing software, and much more.

Those who succeed are not those with a perceived natural ability, as defined by Carol Dweck's idea of a fixed mindset, but rather those who are willing to adapt, change, and flex along with the needs of their organizations. In my own experience, the one skill you need to develop that will launch you toward your goals is the skill of being a lifelong learner and self-educator. Whatever your industry, whether it is building cities, cultivating coding skills, or designing the latest telecommunications technologies (or anything else), your success will depend on your desire and willingness to develop the personal strengths required to accomplish the task at hand.

Many of the most successful people have had very difficult pathways to the great success they eventually achieved. Richard Branson is dyslexic and did poorly in school. Bill Gates's first business—Traf-O-Data—failed. Fashion designer Vera Wang fell short in her quest to make the U.S. Olympic figure skating team. Steven Spielberg was rejected by the University of Southern California School of Cinematic Arts—not once, but twice. J. K. Rowling was a single mom living on welfare when she wrote the first Harry Potter book. Walt Disney was fired by a newspaper editor who said that he "lacked imagination and had no good ideas."

All of our great business and creative heroes and heroines have experienced failure—some of them many times over. But they never gave up. They had the grit and the determination to succeed, regardless of the challenges that faced them. They learned from their failures, and they used what they learned to get ever closer to achieving their goals.

I have no natural gifts as an athlete or as an engineer, but regardless of their absence, I have cultivated the opportunity to thrive as both. My ability to thrive and to live out opportunities that are beyond my wildest dreams—and that are exciting to me every day of the week—is the direct result of my linking my goals to fuel, fire, blaze objectives. I maintain my drive by having a toolset that can break overwhelming problems and projects into meaningful components that I can then process and execute.

There is no accounting for innate ability. Hard work, dedication, and a willingness to learn new skills as appropriate will be the key to success. In order to stay focused using the fuel, fire, blaze hierarchy, develop skills (fuel) to support your blaze goal and step away from relying only on what you already know. This will launch you forward toward your goals.

••• LESSONS •••

- To achieve your highest-level blaze goals, be mentally tough, be persistent, and persevere over a sustained period of time.

- Practice self-control, the voluntary regulation of your behavioral, emotional, and attentional impulses.
- Cultivate a growth mindset, a belief that your abilities can be developed through dedication and hard work.
- Improve your grit by focusing on five areas: courage, conscientiousness, follow-through, resilience, and excellence.
- Be a lifelong learner. You always have room to improve or to learn something new that can help you achieve your goals, and the goals of your organization.

CHAPTER 5

ABIDE THE ROOT LINE

. . . .

PART OF THE ISSUE OF ACHIEVEMENT
IS TO BE ABLE TO SET REALISTIC GOALS,
BUT THAT'S ONE OF THE HARDEST
THINGS TO DO BECAUSE YOU DON'T
ALWAYS KNOW EXACTLY WHERE YOU'RE
GOING, AND YOU SHOULDN'T.

—George Lucas

In long-distance road events, we talk about something called the root line. The *root line* is the shortest possible distance that the course can be run. If you do not run the shortest possible distance, you are expending unnecessary time and energy to achieve the same result. If you take turns that are wider than the root line, you are adding distance. A marathon is 26.2 miles by its shortest path. You can add distance, but you can never decrease it.

With this in mind, most elite runners focus on running the tangent, taking the shortest path whenever possible. There is no reason to take a wide turn when a tight turn will do. There is no reason to use ten words when one will do. The idea is to make every action have a high impact—whether in business, in your career, or in life—by focusing your efforts on the goal at hand and running the root line.

FINDING FOCUS IN A DISTRACTED WORLD

Achieving your goals, no matter what they may be, requires focus. When you work toward achieving a goal, you first complete a small task, then move on to the next task, and then to another, working through all the tasks, one after another, required to achieve your goal. However, as we know all too well, there are many things around us that are competing for our attention, and when we lose focus, this can get in the way of achieving our goals. Instead of tackling the next task required to meet our goal, distractions may cause us to put the task aside and do something else entirely—for a few minutes, a few days, or forever.

Interruption science refers to the study of distractions and interruptions. While the data surrounding our current state of technology-connected distraction remain incomplete and in a state of flux, the majority of studies are finding that we are becoming increasingly distracted at work. The more distracted we get, the farther we get from the root line. We expend unnecessary time and energy to achieve the same result, or perhaps a result that is significantly less than what we had desired or hoped for.

Dr. Gloria Mark, associate professor at the Donald Bren School of Information and Computer Sciences at the University of California–Irvine, who studied workplace interruptions, initially found that "the average amount of time that people spent on any single event (excluding formal meetings) before being interrupted or before switching was about three minutes." Dr. Mark then grouped tasks into related "working spheres" and measured how long it took for people to switch from one sphere to another following interruptions of all types. Using a broader definition of *concentration*, she found that employees "worked 12 minutes and 18 seconds in a working sphere before switching."[1]

The question is: Are the kinds of interruptions that Dr. Mark observed in her research positive or negative for the workplace? Obviously, if you are a fighter pilot flying solo in an aerial battle, you need to stay very focused, and how you respond to interruptions or distractions can mean the difference between life and death. Few of us work in environments that are that intense, but most business-people do have to be able to focus for prolonged periods of time if they are to successfully complete high-level projects, to consistently expend their best efforts, and to be effective in their jobs.

Cathy Davidson of Duke University explains that the maximum length of uninterrupted human concentration before we need a break is 20 minutes. In an interview in *Harvard Business Review*, Davidson described how our minds need occasional distractions in order to perform well. Says Davidson, "So those little breaks when you turn attention away and back are actually like refreshers for your brain."[2]

But, while research shows that occasional distractions or inter-ruptions in our work routines, perhaps every 20 minutes or so, are a positive thing for our overall effectiveness and performance, it's clear that when distractions or interruptions occur more frequently—when they begin to overwhelm us, or when they become more than brief refreshers for our brains—we're not abiding the root line, and our performance suffers.

A critical change in work distractions is that today's technology allows for infinite self-distraction. As recently as 10 years ago, if you were planning a vacation, you could check the Internet for flights and the prices of airlines and hotels, read about the sights to see and restaurants to visit in any location around the globe, and that was about it. Today, you can also see what your friends on Facebook might have posted about the city; read reviews of every store, restaurant, and hotel; communicate with locals about their suggestions; and even rent a house or apartment using Airbnb. While all this additional information may be useful, it takes time to wade through it, and it may fall into the category of self-interruption, which Dr. Mark says accounted for about 44 percent of total distractions in her study.

Research by harmon.ie found that the majority (57 percent) of interruptions on the job were the direct result of e-mail, social networks, text messaging, instant messaging, and switching windows among different computer tools and applications. Says harmon.ie CEO Yaacov Cohen, "Information technology that was designed at least in part to save time is actually doing precisely the opposite."[3] The harmon.ie study also found that 53 percent of employees waste at least one hour a day as a result of all distractions. Not only that, but the employees surveyed indicated that they were able to work only an average of 15 minutes before being interrupted by their digital devices.[4]

While employees of all ages are digitally distracted on the job, participants tend to skew to younger, more tech-savvy workers. Research on the topic shows that employees born between 1980 and 1985 are digitally distracted almost twice as much of the time as those born between 1960 and 1969. And where do all these distractions take them? Primarily to the Internet.[5] Certainly, there have always been distractions in the workplace—this is nothing new. The classic distractions of talking on the phone with friends or chatting with an office neighbor about TV shows or last night's activities has been in part replaced by mobile phones, texting, and other digital means of communication.

While digital device distractions have grown exponentially, they are only one of the sources of job-related distractions, many of which have been part of the workplace for decades, if not centuries. When Ask.com asked 2,060 U.S. adult full-time employees what they consider to be their greatest distractions on the job, 63 percent cited "loud colleagues," with 40 percent of survey respondents saying that they would get more work done if coworkers didn't stop by their offices or desks to chat.[6]

When distractions become overwhelming, then the effect is decidedly negative—on the employee, on coworkers and teams, on customers and vendors, and on the businesses for which they work.

LAUNCHING BLIND AMBITION

When I was in the process of launching my company, Blind Ambition, there was a day when the hustle had gotten the better of me. I felt discouraged and defeated. I was at home—nowhere near the gym, nowhere near my desk—in bed with the covers pulled over my head. I called my number-one lifeline: my aunt, Janet P. Munson.

I explained my situation to her. I have always had a habit of diving into the deep end headfirst. I had factored in the financial burden.

I had factored in insurance and security. But what I hadn't factored in was the sheer fatigue. As a fledgling public speaker, I was traveling a few times a month. Traveling so much made it hard to train. I felt that my goals were in conflict. I needed more time to train, and that required drastic action. I quit my traditional 9-to-5 job. To support myself as a speaker, I was going to have to pay my dues and spend some time working cheaply in order to create a referral business. To do that, I had to take any opportunity I could get.

My aunt posed the question, "How much utility do you think there is in the world for an unmotivated motivational speaker?" I do not consider myself a motivational speaker, but despite that, her point hit home. If I was going to talk publicly about goal achievement, then I had better keep my eye on my own goals. Changing the way persons with disabilities are perceived is my highest-level goal. To make that happen, I needed to eat and sleep—and take care of myself.

My secondary goal was to provide support for my sister's wedding in August 2014. This required money, time, love, and energy. Finally, my tertiary goal was to maintain my ongoing professional development to ensure that I would always have the skills and the money I needed to support myself. I hope to always be developing as a speaker, engineer, and project manager. How to keep all the balls in the air, as we all are required to do, is a challenge that warrants a toolset.

In a perfect world, our goals would exist in a vacuum. The unfortunate truth is that our goals have to coexist with our basic needs. Inevitably, we are faced with competing secondary and tertiary goals, with each activity demanding a slice of our precious time and attention. How often do we feel as if we are swimming in a dishwasher—being bounced around from priority to priority?

I used to feel that success in one facet of my life necessarily meant poor performance in another facet. I felt that being successful at more than one goal could be achieved only through 20-hour workdays and endless brute-force efforts.

I felt ruled by push and pull—a push on one meant a pull on the other. This tug of war took a toll on my health. I have since learned the value of focused effort. The good news about focus is that it can be learned. And not only your focus but your willpower can be trained—just like a muscle. You can set yourself up for success by investing in routines and habits that make work easier.

The other bit of good news is that multitasking is contradictory to focused effort. You can focus on more than one thing in life; you just need to focus on them one at a time. Take your focus and serialize your activity. Budget your time in such a way that at certain times or during certain hours of the day, you focus on the fuel, fire, blaze hierarchy for a particular goal.

How do you handle secondary and tertiary goals? Only in a perfect world do we really have the freedom to focus on one fuel, fire, blaze hierarchy to the exclusion of all others. If I were not on track to pay my rent, maintain my relationships, and develop and sustain my life, training for the Paralympics would be even more daunting. If I could truly just focus on the one goal and trust that my needs would be met, I am certain that the pressure would subside.

When I suggest that you run the root lines, what I am saying is that you need to use your primary fuel, fire, blaze hierarchy to determine whether there are any actions you are taking on a regular basis that are not supporting your goals. Are there any obligations you have that are not advancing your goals? These might be things that you are doing simply out of habit. If these actions do not support your hierarchy, then clean house. Remove any extra turns and conserve the energy that could be better spent on one of your fuel goals.

In 2009, I was working full-time at Microsoft. For most people in the information technology industry, this would be a dream job—the top goal after working for years at much smaller companies. However, things were quite different for me. Instead of reveling in my good fortune, I was in the process of questioning everything, from my career choice, to my choice of employer, to my life's purpose. This is not unusual; most people go through a midlife crisis at around the age of 45 when they question what they have devoted their lives to, and then sometimes make major realignments in their careers, families, and friends. What *was* unusual was that I was just 27 years old—nowhere near my midlife.

I felt that engineering might not be right for me, and that corporations like Microsoft were not the right fit for me. I had begun investigating careers in the nonprofit industry, particularly charities that work to deliver access to clean water in the developing world. I was at a major crossroads in my life, and I didn't really appreciate at the time just how much of an effect the decisions I would soon make would have on my future. My arrival at this key juncture was the direct result of a life-changing journey I had made two years earlier.

In 2007, I went on a four-week trip to Tacloban in the Philippines, an area that was devastated in November 2013 by Haiyan, the strongest typhoon in recorded history. Most of the Philippines is dirt poor, and Tacloban was no exception. I volunteered at an orphanage. I was the only white American in the village. After turning my own life from a downward spiral to an upward trajectory, I felt I had so much to give that it would have been irresponsible of me not to contribute to the global community. I felt inspired to travel and to donate time and money wherever possible and in whatever way I could.

I soon became aware of what life was really like in a developing country, and it wasn't pretty. I stayed in a two-room house with corrugated metal walls that 15 people called home. Like most Americans, I was used to a ton of personal living space, so it took me a day or two to adjust to the tight quarters. But despite the financial challenges that they clearly suffered, the people there had a strong sense of community and family that I immediately came to love and appreciate. They made the best of what they had and were happy.

The orphanage had 50 kids, all under the age of five years old. It was a real wake-up call for me. These kids were barely surviving—there was no socialization or care—and the two staff members were doing what they could with minimal resources. The children with disabilities were in particularly bad shape. The orphanage had oversized cribs—cages, really—for the kids with special needs. It was heartbreaking to have a firsthand introduction to true desperation and survival.

Those kids had nothing. My favorite memory is how elated they were to receive dental floss. They would take a long piece, tie it to a flying beetle, and then fly the insect around like a kite. It was better than a new gaming console. I helped the toddlers with walking practice; I held their little hands as they learned to balance for the first time.

My official volunteer vacation was supposed to be 4 hours a day. I was so enthralled with the experience that I stayed 16 hours a day for at least a month. I eventually had to return home to my job at Microsoft, but I returned with a newfound appreciation for the life of relative luxury that I enjoyed. I reveled in how clean and soft all my things were, and how safe I was in my house, with doors that locked. I felt blessed to be so removed from daily hardship.

I also had a new reverence for humanitarian efforts. While I greatly appreciated my luxury, I had begun to feel unfulfilled. I was contemplating a career that could balance my need for financial security with my aspiration to participate in humanitarian efforts. A career in the nonprofit world seemed to be a good fit for me, so I enrolled in an evening degree program in executive nonprofit leadership at Seattle University. My intent was to prepare to become the CEO or executive director of a nonprofit eventually.

In 2009, after enrolling in graduate school, I decided to enter my first triathlon, IRONMAN Lake Placid. At the time, I did not understand the magnitude of the effort required to compete in an IRONMAN as compared to a marathon.

I was working a full-time job at Microsoft, attending graduate school in the evenings, and training for the IRONMAN. I was completely overcommitted—I had wandered very far from the root line. Looking back, I'm not sure how I survived that time, but I did. I was on a 4:00 a.m. to 1:00 a.m. nonstop schedule.

I was successful in both IRONMAN Lake Placid and IRONMAN Texas, but my success was not without cost. After the May 2011 IRONMAN Texas event, I competed in the World Championships in September 2011. Being stretched so thin left me exhausted. Soon after my return from that event, I crashed with adrenal fatigue syndrome. I went from sleeping 3 hours a night to wanting to sleep 14 or 15 hours a night. It took me about two years to fully recover.

The lesson I learned was that I needed to focus on my blaze goals. If athletics was to be my focus, then I needed to find a career that would support my athletics. I had to pay the bills, just like everyone else. You don't have the option of choosing not to make money. So I decided to launch my own business: Blind Ambition. Blind Ambition gave me a sense of purpose by helping others in their pursuit of goal achievement. It also allowed me the flexibility to get the high-quality workouts that I needed in order to achieve my athletic goals while getting more rest. I felt good about it.

By using the fuel, fire, blaze goal achievement hierarchy, I was able to identify the investments I was making each day that did not enhance my quality of life.

Whatever your blaze goal is, do some reflection on the efforts you are making. Being busy doesn't mean that you are getting closer to your goal—in fact, you can be getting much farther away from it. I often see people in a push-pull lifestyle, which makes it harder instead of easier for them to achieve their highest goals.

Some items that are tangential are necessary. We don't always have a choice. For those items, I would say that if something is supportive of your fuel, fire, blaze hierarchy, then put your heart into it. If it is not supportive, but it is necessary, then just do what it takes to complete the task. Your level of investment is always within your control. Sometimes it is valid to do just enough.

The unfortunate truth is that goals can't live in a vacuum. We have our primary, secondary, and tertiary goals. My response to this is to prioritize. Your primary goal is the most important one of all, and once you figure out what it is, then you have to determine what actions you have to take in order to support it. These actions are nonnegotiable. For example, if your primary goal is to raise healthy, happy children, then you can't not feed the kids. You need to set aside time during your day to accomplish the actions necessary to raise healthy, happy children.

Do the same for your secondary and tertiary goals. Develop a fuel, fire, blaze hierarchy for each. Then use all of that information to budget your time accordingly.

Putting the Root Line to Work

My primary blaze goal is to change the way people with disabilities are perceived in society by setting an example of success in athletics that's on a par with that of able-bodied elite athletes. My secondary blaze goal is to take all that experience and drive to help others achieve their own highest-level ambitions. My tertiary blaze goal is to help move Mozido forward as an advisor to the company's head of engineering. While managing multiple demanding blaze goals, I find abiding the root line to be key in eliminating waste and creating an environment of productivity by cultivating space for focused effort.

How do I accomplish this?

First, I divide my day or week into blocks of time. I then plan a clear objective for what I hope to accomplish within each of those blocks. For example, if I dedicate 9:00 a.m. to 11:00 a.m. to engineering, I follow my fuel, fire, blaze hierarchy to ensure that I focus on that goal. I set a clear objective or deliverable that I anticipate completing during that block of time. This could be the completion of comprehensive research on existing infrastructure in a new market, it could be performing a gap analysis on a technology that our organization has not yet implemented but may have a use for in a new market, or it could simply be the goal of catching up on communication. The goal must be specific and reasonable for that amount of time.

Some people think that they can multitask effectively, keeping their focus on multiple tasks simultaneously. In reality, this is unlikely to be the case. According to research conducted by the French medical research agency Inserm in 2010, there is a limit to how many tasks the human brain can process at once. This limit? Just two. Any more than that, and the likelihood of errors increases. In his experiments, Stanford University researcher Clifford Nass found that chronic multitaskers used their brains less effectively than those who focused on a single activity at a time. So, instead of switching back and forth between tasks every minute or two, he suggests dedicating 20 minutes to a single task, then moving on to the next one.[7]

Keep in mind that when you are shifting your attention between two objectives, you are at most 50 percent effective. To abide the root line is to maintain focus, eliminate waste, and move forward. The principles I use in order to abide the root line are as follows:

1. *Map the path.* For each of your blaze goals, write down what high-level activities you need to carry out in the short term to move you toward your fire milestones. Once you have listed some high-level activities, identify any steps or activities that can be eliminated or postponed. Reduce waste at the beginning to make yourself more efficient. For my blaze goal of enabling opportunities for my organization to be the first to market, it is important that I understand compliance, the existing infrastructure, and our competitors. It is not important that I understand governmental infrastructure, educational systems, and nonrelevant demographic details. While the pursuit of these bits of information feels like it

adds depth to my research, it does not advance the case for a go/no-go decision on the infiltration of new technology into a mobile market. As a result, I can reduce waste by eliminating these steps in the first phase.

2. *Link activity to goals.* Detail for yourself the key objectives that can be accomplished that are linked to your blaze goal. Be sure to keep an ongoing list for your multiple priorities, that is, your multiple blaze goals. For my blaze goal of delivering new opportunities in emerging markets for Mozido, the activities include research, making new contacts, and competitive analysis.

3. *Map a block.* Review your daily schedule to identify opportunities to block off time for yourself for focused effort. You will be amazed at how much you can get done in even 30 minutes when you are focused. Identify what progress you can make toward the activities listed in each block. Each block of time should have a clear objective.

In order to navigate a landscape in which there are multiple high-priority items successfully, I dedicate myself to abiding the root line in managing the utility of my time. To excel as an engineering advisor at Mozido, my blaze goal is to deliver the assessment of technology and proposed solutions as thoroughly and in as timely a manner as possible to enable my organization to actualize a new opportunity in an emerging market. My fire for this objective is quality research deliverables, comprehensive conversations with key stakeholders, responses to requests for proposals, and coordination of technical solutions. The fuel to accomplish these objectives is self-education on new technology and markets, research into competitive solutions, and facilitating ongoing communication.

Abiding the root line requires carving out time for focused effort, setting clear goals, holding yourself accountable for deliverables on specific goals, and maintaining forward motion with the least amount of waste at all times.

I am often asked: Once you have set the goal hierarchy, how do you balance all your different goals? First, prioritize and do away with anything that doesn't fit; this should free up some time. Budget sufficient amounts of time to achieve your goals. In my personal life, my primary goal is to be good to my family. As a result, I specifically set aside time during the week that is focused on calling them, e-mailing them, or helping them with whatever they need. During these budgeted hours, there is no talk or thought of training or work. In these hours, the only thing that matters is being a good family member.

For my secondary goals, the hours before work and after work—from 5:00 to 8:00 a.m., and again from 5:00 to 8:00 p.m.—are budgeted just for athletics. This time is dedicated to everything it takes to move myself forward as an athlete.

Last but not least, I focus on my tertiary goal of career from 9:00 a.m. to 5:00 p.m., with extended hours for continuing education carved out when necessary. There are two major times in my life for continuing education. One is immediately after race season. For a month or two, I take a few hours out of athletics and dedicate them to learning. The other is as required, depending on opportunities.

The amount of time is important, but what is more important is the *use* of that time. *This* is your efficiency. If you work better in a quiet place without distractions, then find a way to create that environment for yourself. If there is anything within your power that you can do to make yourself more efficient, then by all means make investments in whatever it is that will set you up for success.

If you need to turn off your smartphone in order to focus on your work or communicate with coworkers more effectively, then turn off your devices and reduce those distractions in your life. Make your time impactful and purposeful, no matter what that means to you.

I keep hearing a variety of platitudes about goal achievement: "Goals aren't big enough," "People know how to set goals but not how to achieve goals," or "There should be less talking and more doing."

I couldn't disagree more.

No goal is too small. All that matters is that the goal is important to you as an individual. Do not fall into the trap of setting goals in order to impress others. Do not fall into the trap of living according to the judgment of others.

Our primary, secondary, and tertiary goals matter. There is value in acknowledging the incremental goals along the way. I'm a big believer in the power of positive psychology. Happiness leads to success, not vice versa. Success will not necessarily lead to happiness. Celebrate and take pride in all the incremental victories along the way. One of my most important accomplishments was the first mile I ever ran. No one but I was moved by this, but for me it was life changing. In running that first mile, I proved to myself that I was capable of things I hadn't yet imagined. I proved to myself that I wasn't that fragile. All those who had said that my efforts would be an exercise in failure were wrong. What may have appeared to be a small goal, or a goal that wasn't big enough or important enough, set me on a path to prioritize and value my own health—a path to believe in myself and to feel a renewed sense of confidence and self-worth.

After I completed my first mile, I got it into my head to run a half marathon. I trained with a few friends and generally enjoyed the process. I saw major improvements in my fitness and quality of life. I was thrilled to feel that I was more in command of my future. But I had no idea how to set a time goal. I had never timed a mile and had no idea how to go about training. I just kept running solid, slow miles. Roughly a week prior to my race, the 2002 Portland Half Marathon, I overheard someone else who was planning to run the same race. She said her goal was 90 minutes. I decided that my goal was also 90 minutes, based on nothing more than what I had overheard from a seasoned runner.

When the day of the race came, I had a solid performance with a time of 1 hour 45 minutes, just 15 minutes over my goal. Based on sighted able-bodied standards, this would have been on track to qualify for the Boston Marathon. Still, I was disappointed. I was sad. I felt like a failure. Why? Because I had set myself up for failure by setting a goal that was unreasonable. This was a goal that was uninformed by data or an understanding of the task at hand. It was a goal that was based on someone else's expectations. Goals are valuable only if they are informed by data that are specific to you. Adopting someone else's goals may set you up for failure.

When you are setting a goal, do some research on what data points will inform that goal. For example, in my case, a better understanding of my current mile times would have been a good metric. Setting my goals by eavesdropping and because I wanted to fit in with the community of serious runners was a mistake. I denied myself the opportunity to celebrate a strong finish in my first half marathon. I lost the opportunity to enjoy a major positive life transformation. I positioned myself to feel nothing but disappointment after all the hard work I had dedicated to my training and the good results I had realized. Feeling that let down is no recipe for long-term success.

Don't set your goals based on someone else's strengths or weaknesses. Set your goals based on *your own* history, experience level, available time, and access to information. To those who preach less talking and more doing, remind them that ignoring is an action—and then ignore them. Think it through. Set yourself up for success by thinking through your plan. Plan in milestones along the way to celebrate how far you've come toward your goals. Do not pass up opportunities to feel good about what you've accomplished. Those small incremental victories can put you on a new and improved path of self-worth, hopeful living, and appreciation of your own efforts as meaningful.

• • • LESSONS • • •

- Avoid expending unnecessary time and energy by running the root line—the shortest possible distance that you can go.
- To stay on the root line, keep your focus on the task at hand and avoid the everyday distractions of work and life, many of which are constantly competing for your attention.
- To optimize your performance, take short breaks every 20 minutes. This allows you to refresh your brain.
- Put away your digital devices (smartphones, tablets, phablets, and so on) to avoid the distraction of e-mail, text messaging, social networks, instant messaging, and so forth.
- To make time to accomplish the goals you set for yourself, divide your day or week into blocks of time. Then plan a clear objective for what you hope to accomplish within each of those blocks.

- Multitasking is a myth. Instead of trying to juggle multiple tasks simultaneously, dedicate 20 minutes to a single task, then move on to the next one.
- Abide the root line in completing your goals by (1) mapping the path, (2) linking activity to goals, and (3) mapping a block.
- Don't set goals to impress others. Set only goals that are important to you personally and that you fully support and intend to accomplish.
- When you set a goal, do the research on what data points will inform that goal. Make sure that the data are specific to *you*.

CHAPTER 6

Don't Stop Until You Cross the Finish Line

. . . .

Hold yourself responsible
for a higher standard than
anybody else expects of you.

—Henry Ward

We are all accountable for our own ability to achieve our highest potential. So often we are faced with choices that can help us move either toward or farther away from the goal. The task at hand is to stay focused on the end goal and lock onto it until follow-through is complete. To follow through requires focused effort and commitment, but above all it requires a willingness to be honest with yourself.

Training for IRONMAN Lake Placid required countless hours working out on the stationary bike—a race bike on a trainer. At the time, I was living in Seattle, and the endless hours of rain made it difficult to get out on the tandem with my fearless guide Rebecca. At the time, the only tool I had was a heart-rate monitor that beeped if I was either above or below a set zone. I couldn't set the zones myself, so they were always a little off, depending on which sighted person I had recruited to set them most recently.

It's important to have a heart-rate monitor—or, better yet, a power meter—that provides real-time feedback on the effort level or watts you are expending. The question is: How hard are you really working when no one is looking? Remember that the only person who can be helped or harmed by your level of effort or lack thereof is *you*. Still, most of us don't work as hard when we're behind closed doors as we do when we're in front of others. That is human nature.

PROCRASTINATION AND FOLLOW-THROUGH

Setting goals and having aspirations for achieving good things in your business, your career, and your life is all well and good, but if you can't or won't follow through on them—move them forward to completion—then all your hard work and effort is likely to be for naught. Not only will you not achieve your goals, but you may be left psychologically injured after your "failure," with lowered self-esteem, decreased self-confidence, a belief that you're "just not good enough," and other negative feelings that will linger as you try to complete new tasks or goals.

So why are some people able to cross the finish line routinely while others are not? Why do some people seem to achieve their goals easily and consistently, while others can never seem to bring them about? There has been a great deal of scientific research into the nature of task completion, and why some people abandon tasks before they complete them—or don't even start them. One particular focus of this research is procrastination.

In its simplest form, procrastination is putting off doing something until a later time—a few minutes, a few hours, a few days, or much longer. As we all know, when we procrastinate, we are getting no closer to accomplishing the tasks we should be working on, and these deferred tasks may actually move us backward when it comes to achieving certain goals we have set for ourselves as other tasks push their way to the front of the line.

Psychologist Albert Ellis described the nature of procrastination this way:

> You foolishly delay, you put it off and again and again. Why? Because you (stupidly) think, "I'll do it later." It will be better and easier if I do it later. Or you think (idiotically!) "I have to do it perfectly or else I'm a no good, and inadequate person! So I'll do it later.[1]

Of course, we all procrastinate from time to time. Taking an occasional break from a prolonged focus on a particular task can actually enable us to perform better in the long run by giving our brains the quick break that we need if we are to maintain our focus over an extended period of time. However, when we procrastinate when it comes to taking on or completing the tasks that are most important to us, then we may never cross the finish line at all, or we may eventually cross it, but late or with incomplete results.

Studies show that in 1978, only 5 percent of Americans admitted that they were chronic procrastinators. That figure has since risen to approximately 26 percent of Americans today. In addition, 40 percent of people surveyed have experienced a financial loss as a result of their procrastination, and at least 20 percent have allowed procrastination to take such a hold on their lives that it has put their jobs, their relationships, and their health at risk. While some people certainly enjoy the adrenaline rush that accompanies getting a task done at the last minute—after procrastinating on it for some time—most find that procrastination has a negative impact on their happiness. When the Procrastination Research Group asked, "To what extent is procrastination having a negative impact on your happiness?" 46 percent of respondents reported "very much" or "quite a bit," and 18 percent reported that procrastination has an "extreme negative effect" on their lives.[2]

So why do we procrastinate, and why do some of us procrastinate more than others?

Scientists have found evidence that there is a physiological basis to procrastination, and while other factors, including psychology, environment, and upbringing, also play a role, you may already be wired to procrastinate, whether or not you want to. In people who procrastinate more than others, the limbic system of the brain—which generally runs on automatic, is well connected to the brain's pleasure center, and, in the words of psychology professor Timothy Pychyl, is biased toward "immediate mood repair"—dominates the prefrontal cortex, which is the executive area of the brain that gets things done.[3] However, to get things done, we must make a conscious effort to get the prefrontal cortex engaged. For many of us, this is much easier said than done.

Aside from our physiology, there are any number of reasons why we may choose to procrastinate. These include:

- A deep-seated fear of failure
- Feeling overwhelmed by the enormousness of the task
- Lacking the focus needed to stay on task
- Resentment at being assigned the task or goal in the first place
- A desire to avoid doing a task that is overly difficult or unpleasant
- Unclear or fast-changing goals

Fortunately, you don't have to be a victim of procrastination. You can take positive action to defeat it. Here's a seven-step approach to breaking your procrastination habit and enabling you to cross the finish line and achieve the goals you set for yourself:

1. Identify your most important priority.
2. Determine what the first step in working toward the completion of your most important priority is.
3. Make a commitment to start your effort at a definite day and time and to continue this effort for a specific period of time—anywhere from five minutes to five hours or more. Record it on your calendar.
4. Break your task into manageable pieces that can be completed quickly and easily. As you complete these small steps, you will build momentum toward accomplishing your larger tasks and goals.
5. Break the ice by starting your first step at the exact date and time you set on your calendar—not a minute later.

Avoid interruptions that will keep you from starting your task.

6. Continue working on your task for the period of time you set for yourself on your calendar. If you find yourself getting distracted from the task, then reset yourself and reengage in the task as quickly as you possibly can.

7. If you continue to procrastinate, then reassess the task and its relative position in your list of priorities. Is completing it really that important to you? Why or why not? Are there other priorities you should be focused on instead?

Once you get beyond the natural tendency to procrastinate, and you break the ice and get started on your task, how can you improve your follow-through—your commitment to not letting up until after you cross the finish line? I suggest the following approach:

- Set a definite amount of time each day that you will devote to completing your task.
- Tell others about your task or goal, and ask them to check in with you to see how you're doing on it.
- Create an environment that is as free of distractions as possible.
- Just do it. The moment you start working on your task is the moment when all your doubts and excuses will evaporate.
- When you're on a roll, go with it. Don't switch tasks or take a break until your inspiration ebbs.
- Reward yourself when you accomplish specific milestones on the way to completing your task or goal. Take a walk,

have some ice cream, or celebrate in some other small, but meaningful way.

The IRONMAN Experience

When I was training for IRONMAN Lake Placid, a typical Saturday consisted of a six-hour bike ride on my trainer followed by a two-hour run on the treadmill, a total of eight hours of hard work—all to travel absolutely no distance! The life of an aspiring elite blind triathlete is not so different from the life of an aimless sighted hamster. As you might imagine, the battle was more psychological than physical. Physically, my body was conditioned for the task. Mentally, I was bored. I had minimal feedback, and at some point, I even ditched the feedback. I was putting in the time but not the effort required to achieve my goals. I was speaking to a close friend who shared my love of triathlon, and I told her about a book I had recently read. She asked me when I found the time to read, and I answered that I read during all those hours on the trainer bike. She was astonished, and she quickly retorted, "If you can read on the bike, then you aren't working hard enough."

She was right.

It hadn't occured to me that I wasn't putting in the effort. In hindsight, I bet I did put in the effort for the first hour or two, but after that threshold was passed, I mentally checked out. I did not sustain the race level of effort to the finish line. I was training myself to have a strong start and a medium- to low-level finish. It had never occurred to me that I hadn't been working hard enough. I thought the sheer amount of time I was spending in the saddle would be enough to overcome the value of the effort. I was wrong.

Does time spent on a task ever beat effort? No; working longer is never better than working harder. But even better than working harder is working smarter. This is true in any aspect of life—especially in your career and in business. I wasn't working hard or smart, only long. I showed up at my trainer bike every week thinking that I deserved a Medal of Honor just for getting in the saddle and overcoming my boredom. Effort earns the opportunity to participate; hard work achieves goals and earns medals. I realized for the first time that I wasn't setting myself up for a medal, and I was disappointed in myself for not realizing it sooner.

If you want to win on the racecourse, you absolutely must maintain your race level of effort and follow through to the finish. If you want to win in business, you can't let up on your task until you complete it. The race isn't over until you cross the finish line, and the task isn't done until it's done. The results will speak for themselves. You should be within arm's reach of hitting the wall until there is no more wall to hit.

When you let up (even just a little), you take your eye off the prize. And when you take your eye off the prize, you can easily become distracted, become complacent, or lose sight of the goal altogether. If you hope to achieve your highest aspirations, focused and consistent effort is your responsibility. Coasting on a task only undermines your own goal. Every day, ask yourself: What can I do to help myself? What tools do I have to propel myself forward? Have I exhausted all opportunities to further my own goals? Most important, am I pushing myself enough?

During the course of many years of living with the need to overcompensate for my vision loss, I've developed some effective tools and tricks for staying on target. Here are four ways to keep full focus and effort on your goal until it has been won.

Approach 1: Fuel, Fire, Blaze— Answer the "Why" Question

If you are to succeed, you must build and maintain a direct, emotional connection to the goal at hand. To build this connection, ask yourself: Why? Pick something that is central to your life, and then express it in the form of a "why" question; for example, "Why do I go to work?" If your answer to that is simply, "To pay my bills," then prepare to feel underwhelmed each and every day of your life. Just paying your bills is not going to stir the passion within you that you'll need if you are to motivate yourself to achieve your highest goals.

By getting in touch with your emotional self, you will gain a sense of control over your own well-being that will pour into all aspects of your life. I care deeply about financial security. While paying my bills is a key component of that, I feel more emotionally moved by the prospect of cultivating financial security and independence for myself and my family. Paying my bills is a key fuel piece, but the real emotional connection is in creating a better life for myself and the people I love.

My blaze is the prospect of changing the way persons with disabilities are perceived in this world. What a wonderful day it will be when the whole world isn't surprised to see a person with blindness or any other disability do well. The prospect that I could be a player in bringing about this change excites me. This is enough blaze to inspire strategic milestones—events that set a high standard and call attention to persons with disabilities who are succeeding at meeting a high standard. To accomplish the fire and the blaze takes day-to-day effort and focus. It isn't hard to focus when you are excited and motivated. Sometimes the hardest part is just showing up. Having your blaze goal in mind answers the questions: "Why would I show up? Why does this task matter?"

Approach 2: Make an Attempt

Doing anything worthwhile will require effort—there's just no two ways about it. Even so, it is sometimes hard to know where to start. Taking the first step is the hardest part because it's easy to feel intimidated by the enormousness of the task at hand. A well-kept secret, however, is that there is no harm in taking that first step—there is no wrong answer. Whatever place you pick as your starting point will have an associated learning curve. It is said that showing up is 90 percent of completing a task. I agree wholeheartedly. In fact, I would go a step further and argue that even more important than showing up is taking that first stab at something.

Think of all those times when you felt fear or doubt. Think of all those times when you were either trying something new or doing something that you didn't feel comfortable doing. In order to be comfortable, you have to go through a period of skill building that is itself uncomfortable. Make that first attempt. Risk feeling just a tiny bit uncomfortable and out of your wheelhouse. Even if your attempt isn't smooth or graceful, you will be closer to your end goal by cultivating some experience.

Whenever I am feeling overwhelmed by the prospect of starting a task, I make an unprioritized list of three things that need to get done, and then I start to work on checking off each item. Doing this enables me to break out of the inertia that keeps me from moving forward. If you find yourself spinning your wheels, then dial down the pressure by putting together your own list of three things you can accomplish. Then work on each thing, and don't stop or take a break until you have finished all three. Usually I find that this is enough to get me unblocked.

If, after you have completed the three things on your list, your forward momentum is not sufficient to move you closer to your goal, then keep making lists of three more things that need to get done until you see meaningful progress.

Why three things? In my experience, three is the perfect number because it is not overwhelming, but completing three things gives you a sense of accomplishment. I avoid creating long, comprehensive to-do lists. Lists like this require maintenance and can become self-defeating. More often than not, you'll end up wasting focused effort on maintaining your list rather than applying this focused effort to accomplishing the items on the list.

No matter how self-assured or confident we become, we will all have occasions when we will question ourselves. All of us experience occasions of self-doubt. People often credit me with being fearless. All that means to me is that I must hide my fear well. I travel often for work and for races. Imagine having no context and being dropped in a maze where every wall is painted stark white. That is how I feel. I worry that I won't be able to get around. I worry that I won't be able to get out. The tools I have are my memory and walking directions on my iPhone. I pride myself on being self-reliant. Believe me when I say that I am not fearless. I am fearful. I hide it from the outside world because I have long since accepted the need to be able to navigate independently.

When overcoming my internal fear, I just remind myself of all the previous times that I have been faced with that same sense of self-doubt, and how I overcame it by just taking one step after another—one at a time. A thousand small steps forward will eventually equal some sizable progress. It is in these moments of self-doubt that we need to remind ourselves that it is better to have a few failures in our back pockets than to have armfuls of what-ifs. You are always better off for having made the attempt and taken a step toward quieting your fears, rather than backing down before you even started and allowing that fear to transform an opportunity into a what-if. A what-if has no value in any currency. Failure, experience, opportunity, and success are all worth their weight in gold.

Approach 3: Visualize the Result

I've always been a vivid daydreamer. As an adult, I've learned that daydreaming can be a powerful source of motivation. Early in my professional career, my facial expressions were all over the map when I daydreamed. I might look as if I was running from a bear, or as if I'd just seen something hilarious. One way or another, it was readily apparent that I wasn't paying attention to the task at hand. It took me years of conscious effort to be able to turn the visualization off and on as appropriate. Use your imagination as a motivation tool.

A close friend who is a pro triathlete taught me to visualize a successful race in which you meet all your goals. Feel the excitement and the anxiety. Imagine the horn blowing, and see in your mind exactly how powerful you feel in your first stroke of the swim. Visualize how you will navigate people seamlessly through the swim. Take on the turbulent water as if this is what you were born to do. Imagine reaching the end of the swim before you realize it, knowing that it was the best performance of your life. Then move through the first transition, expertly navigating your gear and your fellow competitors. Visualize your bike performance. Run through the course and visualize how you will handle each turn, each hill, and the dismount. Then mentally walk through the second transition and feel what it's like to be on the final leg of the race. Finally, mentally run the run straight through to the finish.

After visualizing a successful race, visualize a race in which you face all your fears. In my case, the water is always a source of vulnerability for me, so I run through one iteration where there is an issue during the swim. I imagine what I will do to handle the situation, no matter what it is. The advantage of these visualizations is, first, that you are preparing your mind to follow through with success, and second, that you are considering tools that you can use to handle the situation if and when something does not go as planned. In a triathlon, it is inevitable that something will not go as planned. This is true for all industries. It's said that if you want to make God laugh, show him your plans. So prepare yourself for the unexpected by mentally running through all scenarios so that when something does happen, your response is trained and automatic.

Approach 4: Get Moving

I won't lie; I *love* coffee. But coffee doesn't always help me focus—in fact, I'm convinced that it sometimes throws me off-track and off my stride. What *does* always help my focus, however, is movement. If you find yourself struggling to get going, and you've tried making a list of three things and executing them to no avail, then find any reason whatsoever to get moving. I guarantee that this will help.

When I found my own focus flagging, I used to get a small group of coworkers together and we'd go outside or to the parking garage and do sets of push-ups. If you aren't up for push-ups, then take a walk. If even that is too much, then focus on doing some isometric holds. Focus on flexing your calves, then your quads. Move up your leg, flexing each set of muscles and holding for as long as you feel is right for you. In short order, you will be awake and alert.

Moving accomplishes several goals. It provides a mini-break from the task at hand while we still feel productive. It rejuvenates our energy systems and our ability to focus by pushing oxygen to the brain. It reminds us of how capable of achieving our goals we are. Moving carves out a little time to chew on a problem. In some cases, it also provides a way for you to bond with your teammates. When my cohorts and I were doing our three sets of push-ups a day, we'd be away from our desks for less than 10 minutes. We had great brief conversations, and we all returned with new energy for accomplishing our work goals. These sets of push-ups were far more effective than any coffee break.

Practice these four approaches as often as possible. Soon they will feel natural to you. We've all coasted from time to time: we feel as if we've done the work when we're in the home stretch, and we celebrate prematurely. Hold strong and stay the course. Keep pushing with maximum focus and intent until the results are seen to be successful. Don't let up just because you're winning—you haven't won until you cross the finish line. Believe me, circumstances can change anytime. Being on top of the world today means that you have the opportunity to practice what life is like in a push situation. Remember that every action you take is the precedent for the next action. If you coast today, then you may coast by accident during crunch time because that is the behavior you've practiced. Practice the focus that is required to accomplish your blaze goals as often as possible, in keeping with your fuel, fire, blaze priorities.

CROSSING THE FINISH LINE AT WORK

Not stopping until you have crossed the finish line means cultivating the tools you need to help you maintain your focus and an energized state until you've finished your task or reached your goal. When we are creating new opportunities for ourselves and for our organizations, we need to learn how to engage this same flow. It's all too easy to succumb to procrastination or to reduce our effort as we near the end of a task. Letting up prematurely does you and your organization a disservice. If an activity is key to your blaze goal, it should be done to the very best of your ability. Practice the necessary maneuvers to maintain drive and motivation.

In your career, your focus needs to stay on your current objective. Set a blaze goal. Determine the fuel and fire milestones. Within a fuel milestone, your flow will be the determining factor for your success. You will need to block out everything that is not helping you focus on the task at hand. This is where mental toughness is cultivated.

While I was at Microsoft, I was given responsibility for an initiative to introduce web accessibility to online advertising. There was a segment of the population that was not being reached by our prospective ads. I understand that you may be thinking that this must have been a good thing for those people, but we were trying to implement ads as a service. For example, as you are passing a coffee shop, you may receive an ad for a discount on its products based on proxemics. I wanted to ensure that people with disabilities had the same opportunity as anyone else to receive cost savings.

In order to convince the Microsoft decision makers to make this investment, I had to make a strong case for the revenue, compliance, and regulations, and also trade-off decisions, that supported an investment in accessibility. I had to present at our weekly war meeting, socialize the idea among upper management, and defend it to a team of peers who were competing for resources. I determined the following fuel, fire, blaze hierarchy: the blaze was to see all services made accessible to the blind and disabled as a step toward full inclusion in all technology and the advantages that technology could offer; the fire was to take any and all opportunities to advocate on these people's behalf; the fuel was the day-to-day battle of bringing attention to inclusion.

My first mistake was overconfidence. I thought that because I had a good idea, all I had to do was present it and the choice would be obvious. I stood in front of our war team, a team of executives who made go/no-go decisions on the future direction of company programs. This team was notorious for grilling and high-intensity questioning. As a developing professional, I stood in front of this team of executives and presented the premise that accessibility is important because it is important to be accessible—offering a huge dose of circular logic. In hindsight, I embarrassed myself. They grilled me on revenue numbers that I didn't have, regulatory compliance details that I didn't know, and trade-offs that would need to be made that I hadn't considered. I had demonstrated overconfidence and a lack of mental toughness that left me floundering toward my blaze goal. I quickly learned that I would need to embrace the principles of mental toughness if I was to make any headway. I had felt intimidated by being in the hot seat. I knew then that in order to succeed, I would have to learn to be comfortable with the feeling of intimidation while learning not to avoid situations that are intimidating.

Abandonment occurs when we lose track of why our day-to-day fuel objectives are important—when we lose sight of what is on the line. This is why it is important for us to have our fuel, fire, blaze hierarchy at hand, so that we can remind ourselves why a particular objective will further our goals.

Defending the inclusion of accessibility gave me the opportunity to demonstrate the ability to stay calm under pressure. This was relatively early in my career at Microsoft, and I had not yet cultivated the confidence to defend my position vigorously. There is a maturity threshold in a career when you are transformed from someone who accepts marching orders into someone who makes suggestions for where to march. I was on the cusp of this empowerment. I had to practice staying cool under pressure when defending my desire to include accessibility in our higher-revenue products. Staying true to the fuel, fire, blaze hierarchy helped me to make strong arguments and appear confident as I defended my initiative. It enabled me to concentrate on what was important and block out other distractions.

I admit that on a few occasions, I battled the temptation to abandon the goal. Standing in front of the war team to defend this cause could be someone else's problem or someone else's crusade. I wanted to work on something that was a little more under the radar and would go unnoticed. To overcome the feelings I had that abandoning the project would be a prudent course of action for the furtherance of my Microsoft career, I reminded myself of what was on the line. I used the principles of mental toughness to help me overcome a desire to abandon the initiative in order to stay focused on my blaze goal.

But that wasn't the only battle I had to fight on an ongoing basis. As I was maturing in my career, but not quite there, I was constantly tempted to procrastinate. I wanted to put off until tomorrow things that could be done today. This was motivated by a sincere fear of failure. My initial overconfidence concerning my attempt to push the accessibility initiative had led me to fall flat. I now felt the fear of feeling humiliated. I struggled to rebound, and to pull the pieces together and maintain drive. It was through my capacity for resilience that I was able to continue the pursuit of my goal of accessibility.

To complete my initiative, I needed executive sponsorship, funding, and dedicated time. I was able to muster the mental focus required by maintaining solid self-awareness. When I was presenting to the war room—or to executives on a one-on-one basis—anytime I was feeling down, I regrouped immediately by keeping my blaze goal top of mind. I practiced self-affirmations and gave myself confidence boosts, reminding myself of projects that had previously gone well. I knew that the only way I could see my blaze goal through to fruition was to maintain self-motivation. I maintained control of my emotions through a combination of concentration, confidence, and a comfort with being uncomfortable.

I engaged with Microsoft's financial department to research our consumer population of persons with disabilities, and I put together the various cost-benefit analyses of the investment. I then consulted with our legal counsel on all relevant laws and potential litigation. I worked with the head of engineering to understand the key trade-offs. If we were to include accessibility, what would we lose as an organization? By learning from my overconfidence, managing my desire to abandon the initiative, and chipping away at the fear that resulted in my procrastination, I was finally able to muster the necessary support for my initiative. Accessibility became part of the checklist for every product before release. After learning to apply the principles of mental toughness to my initiative, I was able to ensure that accessibility would be part of all services offered through the Microsoft Advertising platform.

• • • LESSONS • • •

- Avoid procrastination by recognizing and overcoming the fear of failure, feeling overwhelmed by the enormousness

of a task, lack of focus, resentment at being assigned a task
or a goal, desire to avoid a difficult or unpleasant task, or
unclear or fast-changing goals.

- Breaking large tasks that may seem unwieldy or even
  impossible to accomplish into small, easy-to-accomplish
  tasks builds momentum toward goal accomplishment
  while generating a feeling of success.
- Improve your follow-through by creating an environment
  that is free of distractions and enhances your ability to
  work instead of undermining it.
- When you're on a roll, don't stop! Keep going for as long
  as you can toward the completion of your selected task.
- Reward yourself for reaching specific milestones along
  the way.
- Keep your full focus on your efforts toward achieving a
  goal by:
  - Answering the "why" question
  - Making an attempt
  - Visualizing the result
  - Moving forward

CHAPTER 7

Bet on Yourself

• • • • • • • • • • • • • •

If you're interested, you'll do what's
convenient; if you're committed,
you'll do whatever it takes.

—John Assaraf

We all have people in our lives who, whether intentionally or unintentionally, try to steer us away from doing the things we want to do or are capable of doing, because they hope to spare us the pain of failure. I have a message for these well-meaning people: everyone fails, and it is through failure that we learn the things we need to know if we are to avoid failing again and be able to enjoy the sweet taste of success. Understand that in many cases, what is a breakthrough to you may appear to be a breakdown to the outside world. You must be accountable to yourself if you are to live up to your full potential, which means having some faith

123

in yourself and in your abilities. When you know that what you're feeling is a breakthrough, then muster the courage to welcome risk into your life and bet on yourself.

From 2009 to 2011, I worked full-time at Microsoft while earning a master's degree in the evenings and training for my world record–breaking IRONMAN. The end result was some incredible life experiences and massive exhaustion. I had earned both bragging rights *and* adrenal fatigue syndrome, and I quickly realized that something had to give if I hoped to pursue my blaze goals. In 2012, the decision was made to add triathlon to the 2016 Paralympics. I realized that if I was to be a viable competitor, I needed to align my goals so that there would be less push and pull between the competing demands in my life.

The opportunity to do just that arrived when, as a result of my IRONMAN record, I began receiving exponentially more requests to make presentations at local conferences and schools. I suddenly—and unexpectedly—realized that I might have a future as a professional public speaker, but I also knew that this would require me to take a tremendous risk. I would have to leave behind the comfort of a regular 9-to-5 career with one of the world's largest and most successful software companies and become an independent contractor with an uncertain stream of incoming projects, and with paychecks that might be plentiful one month and missing altogether the next.

Risk Taking and the Fear of Failure

Fear is in our DNA. Our brains and bodies are prewired for it. And while fear can protect us from things that can harm us, such as a wild animal, it can also "protect" us from things that may be good for us.

Take, for example, the fear of speaking in front of a large group of people (glossophobia). While we may be comfortable giving an informal PowerPoint presentation to a handful of coworkers in an office setting, if you put us up onstage in front of 500 people—with the lights in our eyes, a formal introduction, and the applause of an audience that is looking forward to a stellar performance—we may find ourselves paralyzed by fear. Unlike the fear we might feel when we're face to face with that wild animal, there are really no positives to having a fear of public speaking. This fear is likely to cause us to choke and give a poor performance, which will make us even more fearful the next time we're in the same situation. We sweat, we stammer, we fumble with our words, we lose our train of thought—we may even be overcome by nausea or a powerful desire to flee. If you feel nervous speaking in front of a group of people, then you're not alone—approximately three out of every four people suffer from glossophobia.

Similarly, the fear of failure (atychiphobia) has no discernible positives and a mountain of negatives. If you think about it for a minute, you'll realize that we typically don't fear failing at something that we're really good at. For example, if we've put together many reports for the executive team over the years, and we're frankly really good at it, then we're probably not going to worry much, if at all, about failing at that. Instead, what we fear most is the failure that we might experience when we take on a new task or do something that we believe puts us at personal or career risk. For example, your boss might ask you to suggest and implement new approaches to solving an ongoing problem with collecting customer sales data. However, you may find yourself paralyzed by the fear that you're going to screw up the project and look bad—not only to your boss, but to your coworkers and others who may learn of your failure. Fear of failure may prevent us from:

- Trying new solutions to old problems on the job
- Seeking a promotion to a position with greater responsibilities and higher pay
- Challenging the status quo
- Speaking up in meetings
- Volunteering to take on new duties
- Making a presentation to a large group
- Taking creative approaches to solving problems
- Enjoying life, given the massive stress and anxiety that we feel

To succeed in business, career, and life, we must all take risks from time to time, which means that we must face down our fear of failure. This is especially true for women, who numerous studies show are less inclined than men to take risks. But the rewards for women—and men—who face down their fear of failure and take risks are many. As Sandra Peterson, group worldwide chairman of Johnson & Johnson, told *Forbes* magazine in an interview:

> Most women I know who have been successful in business, it's because they've been willing to take on the risky challenge that other people would say, "Oh, I'm not sure I want to do that." If you look at my career, I've taken on a lot of risky roles. They were risky to some people but to me it was, "Wow, this is this great opportunity and it's allowing me to learn new things

and take on a bigger role and a bigger organization." But some people would view that as, "Are you crazy? What do you know about diabetes, or what do you know about washing machines or the food industry or automobiles or the agricultural industry?"[1]

In Peterson's case, facing down her fears and taking risks led her to the top management ranks of a global healthcare giant with annual sales in excess of $71 billion. Think about your own career and your own life through the prism of the question that Facebook COO Sheryl Sandberg asked in *Lean In*: "What would you do if you weren't afraid?" I'll venture that the answer might surprise you.

Facing down your fear of failure and taking risks offers you a much clearer path to achieving your goals than does allowing your fear to overwhelm you and rule your life. But taking risks doesn't mean that you can or should put everything on the line, putting your business, your career, or your life in danger. In fact, it's much smarter to place many small bets on yourself than it is to place one or two large bets. When you place small bets, not only are you putting less at risk, but you can be much more agile, rebounding quickly if one or two of them don't work out the way you had hoped. In fact, failing fast can help you get to your goals more quickly than you imagined.

In his book *Little Bets: How Breakthrough Ideas Emerge from Small Discoveries*, Peter Sims noted:

Failing quickly to learn fast is also a central operating principle for seasoned entrepreneurs who routinely describe their approach as *failing forward*. That is, entrepreneurs push ideas into the market as quickly as possible in order to learn from mistakes and failures that will point the way forward. This is an extremely well-known Silicon Valley operating principle. Howard Schultz's experience building Starbucks illustrates the point. He and his colleagues had to try hundreds of ideas, on everything from nonstop opera music to baristas wearing bowties, to hundreds of different beverages before being able to define the Starbucks experience.[2]

Did Howard Schultz take risks? Without a doubt. Did they pay off for him and his company? Definitely.

If you find that a fear of failure is preventing you from taking risks and doing the things you need to do if you are to achieve your goals, what can you do about it? Here are five things you can do right now:

- *Change your attitude.* Understand that we all fail on the way to achieving our goals, and that the faster you fail, the sooner you will achieve your goals. As long as you learn lessons from your failure, you're on the right path.
- *Worry less about what others think about you.* No one wants his coworkers, friends, and family to see him fail. Not only is it embarrassing, but we don't want to let others down. However, such misplaced worry will only prevent you from ever taking risks or trying something new. Don't worry about what others will think about you if you take risks— keep your eye on the prize.
- *Do your homework.* Remember that success comes to those who put the time into everything that's required to get

them to that point. If you don't do the homework, how
can you expect to pass the test?

- *Don't be afraid to ask others to help and support you.* When
  you enlist the help and support of others, whatever it is
  that you want to do won't seem quite so scary, and your
  chances of success will multiply.

- *Start small.* Take small risks that result in incremental
  victories. Build on those incremental victories to take progressively larger risks and win progressively larger victories.
  As your momentum builds, you'll find that your fear of
  failing will evaporate along with it.

MAKING THE LEAP

In 2012, I made the fateful decision to leave Microsoft to pursue a new career in speaking—establishing my own business, Blind
Ambition. The decision wasn't an easy one, but when I weighed the
pros and cons, I felt that the risk was worth taking. Speaking allowed
me more time for training and more flexibility for races, and if the
demand for my services was any indication, I could make a good living
doing it. So I took the leap of faith, and I made a big bet on myself.

What had been keeping me at Microsoft was a love of my teammates, the enjoyment of financial security, and the excitement of
working on some of the most advanced technology. The enjoyment
I received from my employment pales, however, in comparison to
the excitement I feel when I realize that I might have the opportunity to represent my country in 2016. If I hadn't left Microsoft,
this outcome would not have been a possibility for me.

So I left the job that I had worked so hard for. I had spent years
in school preparing for a career in engineering, and I was ready to

walk away from it. I felt that I was experiencing a breakthrough, but some of the people around me thought I was having a breakdown. Imagine receiving this information: someone you know and love has a successful career in a thriving industry, this person is not getting any younger, and out of the blue she tells you that she is leaving everything behind in order to pursue a career as a professional athlete. I might think that person was having a breakdown, too. I received mixed responses to my decision, which certainly led me to have second thoughts about it. Some people were supportive and others were terrified on my behalf.

I was encouraged and apprehensive all at once, but I knew deep inside that I had to make the attempt. By walking away from my career at Microsoft, I had walked up to the edge of a very high cliff and then jumped off. I knew that when I drove away from the building in which I had worked—with my office packed into a few boxes in the back of the car—I had passed the point of no return.

I have not looked back.

Less than two years later, I have more speaking engagements than I can keep up with, I love my profession, and I have all the time in the world to train. I will be forever thankful that I bet on myself, that I jumped off that cliff. The people you love and care about—your family, friends, and coworkers—will give you all sorts of advice, hoping to turn you away from decisions that might seem overly risky to them. But the only person who knows when your breakthrough will happen is you. I strongly encourage you to face your fears and embrace those breakthrough moments when they arrive in your life.

There is an ever-growing role for conviction in business, that is, for leaders who aren't afraid to have firm beliefs and values. Almost every industry has been disrupted as technological advances have changed our landscape in real time. Therefore, it has become ever more important for leaders not only to bring their traditional organizational and people skills to the table, but to supplement those skills with innovation and creativity. In order to survive, you have to be willing to bet on yourself from time to time. Those who aren't afraid to have convictions and to display them for all to see can differentiate themselves, as the world has less and less real estate available for the yes-men.

If you're not doing what's necessary to keep up with all the change that's going on around you and your business, the status quo will leave you behind. Keeping an eye on the horizon for coming changes, advocating for a strategic vision, and having the conviction to see it through will give you a very real edge in your markets and with both current and prospective customers.

BELIEVE IN YOURSELF

Sometimes it takes a lot of courage to bet on yourself—especially when you're bucking conventional wisdom, when you're going up against the status quo, or when you're put in the position of having to engage in difficult conversations with an employee or your boss. To go all in, you've got to have a command of the facts, you've got to be self-confident, and you've got to be willing to fight for what you know is right.

In the world of software development, there are two major paradigms that are in widespread use. The waterfall method refers to a method of development in which an organization first writes comprehensive specifications and documents to define the requirements for the product, initiates development of the product, and finally runs the product through quality assurance to verify that what was developed meets the requirements in the original document. This methodology worked well for software released in stable environments, where the requirements were understood up front. However, with the onset of lean thinking, which emphasizes developing software at a much faster pace, developers realized that by the time the software was developed using the waterfall method, the requirements were out of date. To respond to this shortfall, the industry has increasingly adopted the Agile method of software development. Using Agile, the objective is to deliver a consumable product at set intervals with requirements that are specific to that feature set. Smaller pieces delivered more frequently ensures both that software meets the current needs of customers and that it is adapting to what can be a fast-changing landscape.

While I was assigned to the Microsoft Ad Center, part of our job was to implement the change from the waterfall method to Agile. In my first year with the organization, we all thrived on the excitement of changing industry standards and the challenge of trying to release a consumable product to our sales force at six-week intervals. This was unprecedented for Microsoft, which had typically taken a couple of years to prepare a consumable product for release using the old waterfall method of software development.

As was to be expected, of course, our first few iterations were challenging. It takes a great deal of focused effort on the part of a lot of people to make the transition from waterfall to Agile successfully—adjusting to the appropriately scoped amount of work in a given period of time, keeping sprints (the six-week cycles leading up to a product release) focused on related feature sets in order to reduce context switching of key developers, and accounting for the increased overhead required for deployment of the product to the world.

We had our first sprint, and, as expected, there were challenges. This first sprint was followed by a few more failed sprints where the specific goals were delayed or the requirements not met. As the new paradigm took hold, however, we experienced a few sprints that were right on target, and we gained confidence in our ability to work effectively within this new system—that is, until we went off the rails a second time, with both missed requirements and delayed deadlines. This was a concern, to say the least. By successfully completing a number of sprints, we had proved that our team could operate well in an Agile development environment. Then going off the rails again gave me the distinct impression that something had changed somewhere along the way. I was given the task of carrying out postmortem examinations of each sprint to understand the reasons for our inconsistency.

I started my task with a group meeting to discuss and get an overall feel for the pulse of the organization. Quickly, a few themes became apparent. First, everyone (in typical Microsoft fashion) was working long hours—usually seven days a week and twelve hours or more a day. On days when deployments occurred, some individuals were at the office overnight and were expected to work through the next day as well. They were feeling pushed to the breaking point.

At this initial meeting, I noted the frustration, the exhaustion, and the resulting hostility toward the change to Agile. I knew that these were all symptoms of a bigger problem. I also knew that Agile was not the problem, as we had proved that we could execute it. I decided that to get to the source of the problem, I would have to meet with individuals and dig a little deeper.

I scheduled a series of one-on-one meetings with everyone on the team: about 50 developers, project managers, and quality assurance engineers. During the course of those meetings, I asked everyone the same open-ended questions. I let them know up front that it was important for them to speak candidly about what they felt was the root of the problem. To my dismay, the answer I heard from everyone I interviewed was virtually unanimous: the problem was with my immediate supervisor. When I originally took on the task, I had intended to be responsible for the postmortem of a system. As it turned out, I became responsible for the postmortem of an individual—my boss.

The consensus was that the members of the team felt that they were being pushed too hard. In successful sprint planning, the team buys into the scope of the work it can deliver during the six-week period. This requirement had been undervalued in our transition, and we had reverted to the waterfall model: a top-down determination of what would be delivered based on unrealistic deadlines.

Although all fingers were pointing at my boss, I knew that he was not wholly responsible for the problems we were facing; there was some groupthink at play as well. I also knew that regardless of the complexity of the situation, my boss had become the face of the problem, the convenient scapegoat. From my perspective, the unrealistic deadlines that the team was facing were coming from someone higher up in the organization than my boss. Unfortunately, he was just the messenger. Considering that my boss had a large say in my future at Microsoft, I felt stuck between the proverbial rock and a hard place. My objective was to uncover the problem and help my team deliver on requirements, improve work-life balance, and get back to a strong cadence of development and delivery. The task had now morphed into giving the person responsible for my success, my boss, the unpleasant feedback that the team members believed that he was to blame. I was at a loss.

I had tremendous respect for my boss, and I knew the pressure that he and the other managers were feeling from the top. I also knew that his intention was to help all of us in our careers by developing our reputation as a team that was able to deliver whatever the higher-ups mandated. His intentions for each individual and for our organization as a whole were good.

Anyone who has ever been given the task of delivering negative feedback to an individual can attest to how challenging it is to offer it constructively. Feelings often get hurt, and communication shuts down. Add to that the complexity that comes with delivering negative feedback up the chain of command—to the hardest-working person you have ever met, who had nothing but good intentions—when some of this feedback was unjustly placed on him because of the team's misperception.

I was feeling way outside of my wheelhouse and my comfort zone, but I also knew that I had to do what was right for my boss, my team, my company, and, ultimately, myself. This meant changing my attitude. I needed to gather my courage, make sure I was in full command of the facts of the situation, and move forward in a way that was sensitive to my boss's need to respond affirmatively to the orders he was getting from above. I needed to bet on myself, and I knew that I couldn't just look the other way when it came to this particular postmortem, as unpleasant as it had personally become for me.

Within the team, an "us-versus-them" dynamic had developed— it was the team versus management. I knew that by adopting an "I'm-in-this-with-you" mentality when it came to my boss, I would be siding with management. This, however, was an occasion for worrying less about what other people thought and more about what I thought. The objective was to improve the situation for the team and for the company. In order to do that, a partnership was necessary.

I could have wrapped up my findings, made a meaningless conclusion, and not rocked the boat. Secretly, that was exactly what I wanted to do. I had worked so hard to get to my position that I knew I would be taking a risk with no clear outcome.

Ultimately, I decided to bet on myself.

That didn't make it any easier. I was afraid, and I felt intimidated, knowing that I would have to communicate to others that my boss, and his bosses, were the reason that our sprints were going sideways. To turn this situation into something constructive, I knew that I would have to find a way to spin this message so that I would be seen as a positive change agent up the chain of command. I also knew that I would need help to do so. Because of the lack of work-life balance since the changeover to the Agile development model, my team had experienced high turnover. Talented, hard-working people were burning out and leaving in droves. Based on these data, I scheduled a confidential meeting with the human resources department to discuss my findings candidly and seek its recommendation.

Our HR representative offered to have the conversation for me. While I appreciated her offer to speak to my boss for me, this didn't feel right to me. Doing the right thing meant having the guts to lay out the facts to my boss. It would not be constructive to offload this challenging task to someone else. But I did ask the HR representative to coach me on the approach that she recommended. I took careful notes and practiced the interaction in my mind. I did my homework in working with HR and following up on the representative's reading recommendations to develop the skill of having difficult conversations. I asked others for help with some specific examples, and in identifying what they expected of managers' behavior in a sprint model versus what they felt was actually happening. I was determined to start small, discussing one problem at a time, during a private one-on-one conversation.

My boss was reliably in his office by 5:30 a.m. every day. While I knew that these early morning hours of uninterrupted work were precious to him, I balanced that against the need to keep this conversation private. Some hardworking, driven people may seem like robots to those they work with, but everyone has a vulnerable side. I wanted to treat the situation with sensitivity. I scheduled a 6:00 a.m. meeting with my boss over coffee. I began by sincerely expressing how much respect I had for my manager's work ethic and his strong command of technology. I said that what I had discovered in my postmortem was completely different from what I had expected to find. I then explained that the team members' perception was that management was pushing unrealistic deadlines, and that this had resulted in resentment within the team. I spoke carefully, using language that was free of blame and encouraged collaboration. I wanted him to know: "I'm with you in this. I am on your side. We have the same goal." After I delivered the news, I asked him how I could help manage this perception.

It was at that moment that I saw my boss's vulnerable side. Hardworking people are still people—they have feelings and emotions. My boss quickly responded, "You started a postmortem of the sprint, and you ended up with a postmortem of me," in a tone that was heavy with deep hurt. I had never felt so awful in a professional setting. Despite wanting to be gentle and constructive, I had missed the mark.

It was clear to me that my manager wanted some time and space to work through what I had just told him. I walked away with a heavy heart, uncertain as to whether or not I had done any good at all—for my boss or for my company. Not only that, but I might very well have done irreparable harm to my career at Microsoft. I found myself wishing that I could go back in time and give this problem to someone else.

My boss canceled all his meetings and left for the day. This was bad. I had never seen him take a day off.

The buzz around the office was that meetings started appearing on everyone's calendars—one-on-ones with my boss. It was the single bravest response I have ever seen in my professional career. My boss had taken the feedback that I had given him, reflected on it, and decided with a mentor that it was the right time for a 360-degree review. In a 360-degree review, you ask deep questions of those you work with, and you should be very open to receiving candid feedback—both good and bad.

On my own calendar, I saw a 6:00 a.m. meeting a week later. My boss bought me a coffee and gave me a remarkably thoughtful card with a $50 gift certificate to Lululemon (years later, I still wear the running shorts I bought with that gift card). He took all the feedback that he had received from the one-on-one meetings and worked with his mentor on a development plan. I noticed changes immediately: he provided more comprehensive explanations of what was behind the deadlines and was candid about the pressures from the top. He showed a new respect for team members' work-life balance, which led to better rapport with the entire team.

I was very moved by my boss's gesture of gratitude, supporting my athletics. He was appreciative of my honesty and sensitivity in a delicate situation. He knew that I had tried my best to be constructive while delivering a hurtful message. We had a long heart-to-heart about how hard it had been to hear, how challenging the 360-degree review had been on a personal level, and his plan for development moving forward. The sense was that everyone would be better off, and that the team would be able to execute better with improved communication and an understanding of market pressures.

I had nothing but admiration for my boss. To this day, I consult with him before I make any major life decisions. My trust in and respect for him is unwavering.

I learned a tremendous lesson through this experience. Knowing that I was doing the right thing for everyone involved restored my confidence. By listening to and trusting myself and quieting my fear of what others might think of me, I was able to bridge the "us-versus-them" divide that had developed on our team. By reaching out to HR for help, I was able to learn new critical skills and deepen a key relationship that would have lifelong benefits. By doing my homework and reading up on how to have difficult conversations, I became a better communicator and, to this day, do not shy away from challenging conversations.

As difficult as it was to do, I am grateful that I bet on myself. The skills and the greater understanding of the power of empathy that I developed through the process have helped me every day in my career. I learned that no matter how tough someone may appear to be, that person assuredly is more sensitive than you realize. I learned that to be open to receiving hard feedback is valiant. And I learned that these most challenging of personal victories are devoid of external validation.

There is no convenient time to jump off a cliff. Throughout my career, I have had many successes and many failures. The successes have reinforced my belief in my instincts and judgment. The failures have given me experience, strength, resilience, and a gut-level understanding that there will be another day. All of us experience fear and self-doubt at various times, but all of us can overcome the obstacles and challenges that we face. It is our willingness to bet on ourselves that makes it possible for us to hone our resilience, create opportunities, and achieve our greatest goals.

Reflect on what you have a genuine conviction for, then take that conviction and create opportunities for yourself. You could invent a life-changing product, or you could find some way to increase your company's top-line revenue or its bottom-line profit. You could initiate something new that has a high impact, or you could spare yourself and your organization further losses by having the guts to stop an underperforming effort before it progresses too far. And you could lift yourself up by demonstrating to the world that you have convictions concerning how you will be perceived—and received.

Be unexpected. Do not follow the pack just because you were told to do so, and evaluate each situation as an opportunity to lead or to follow. Following is part of life, but when you see an opportunity to lead, and it fits into your life goals, by all means, take that opportunity. When you see that the pack is not going in the right direction, then it is your responsibility to speak up and correct it. Speak to your own integrity.

I take pride in being someone who I'd like to work with. One piece of this is having the strength and confidence to speak up. I like the expression "big ear, little mouth"—seeking to understand before you seek to be understood. It is always appropriate to think through your actions. If you have thought the situation through, and you see an error, whether in the family or in a board of directors, respectfully make your case—have the conversation. You'll find that this cultivates trust and confidence in your contributions and demonstrates your investment.

••• LESSONS •••

- To succeed in business, career, and life, we must face down our fear of failure and take risks.
- Change your attitude about failure. We all fail—the key is to learn valuable lessons from those failures that will get you farther along on your path forward.
- Place small bets and fail faster. This will actually get you to your goals more quickly.
- Don't worry about what others think about you—worry about what *you* think about yourself, and take action accordingly.
- Be prepared and do your homework. Success comes to those who put in the work required to achieve it.
- Ask others to help and support you on your path.

CHAPTER 8

LIVE YOUR CORE VALUES

• • • • • • • • • • • • • •

> IF WE ARE TO GO FORWARD, WE MUST GO
> BACK AND REDISCOVER THOSE PRECIOUS
> VALUES—THAT ALL REALITY HINGES ON
> MORAL FOUNDATIONS AND THAT ALL
> REALITY HAS SPIRITUAL CONTROL.
>
> —Martin Luther King Jr.

O ne of the most difficult breakthroughs in my athletic career occurred during a lecture on sports psychology at the U.S. Olympic Training Center in Colorado Springs. The expert who was lecturing that day advocated putting all of your focus into the event once the event has started—use the power of being in the moment with all your mental, physical, and emotional self. That sounds easy until you try to put it into practice.

Thinking and focus are opposite forces—the second you are thinking about anything other than this instant in an event means that you have lost your focus. In other words, do not visualize winning; do not spin cycle while focusing on your race strategy; do not reorganize your shopping list in your mind or get lost in some other thought. Putting all your focus into the event means that you are aware of every fiber of your being in order to maximize your power and the efficacy of your movement.

As I sat there listening to this lecture, I realized that I had always been focused on winning the race—I was always thinking about the next move, not the current move. The next day during swim practice, I tried to focus on a slow-and-steady swim while desperately trying to keep my mind from wandering. It was one of the hardest things I've ever done. It occurred to me that in order to truly be able to leverage the power of focus, you have to practice it—set the entertainment aside, turn your mind off, and cultivate a fire for the present moment. Not only that, but you have to know what your core values and purpose are, and you have to be living and breathing them every day of the week. When your values and purpose aren't in sync with your day-to-day goals, tasks, and actions, then accomplishing those day-to-day goals will be much more difficult, if not impossible.

THE POWER OF VALUES AND PURPOSE

The leaders of today's most successful companies know that there's more to business than just making money. Sure, making money is an important factor in the business equation, but the people who own, run, and work in most companies today also want to make a difference in the lives of others. When companies take the time to define what their values and purpose are, and when the leaders of these companies demonstrate their support for these values and purpose by living them, then employees can and will use them to guide their day-to-day decisions. And when employees are aligned with a company's values and purpose, they will be more engaged in their jobs, and will become more effective and efficient in the process.

We've heard a lot about values and purpose in business, but what exactly are they?

Values are the principles and standards of behavior that a company follows, while a company's *purpose* is its reason for being. So while a company might follow and promote certain values, such as honesty, transparency, and happiness, its purpose might be to provide customers with the highest-quality products, or to provide its shareholders with the highest possible level of return on their investment. *Core values* are the values that a company's leadership team considers to be the most fundamental and important to the organization, and that therefore should never be violated or ignored.

When it comes to values and purpose, there are no right or wrong answers (every company will have its own unique set), and they may change over time as the company's culture changes. And while values and purpose may overlap from company to company—there are only so many different values and purposes to go around, after all—they generally differ in subtle, and sometimes not-so-subtle, ways.

Online shoe retailer Zappos has made a point of living and promoting widely its set of 10 "Zappos Family Core Values." The company uses these core values to develop its culture, its brand, and its business strategies. As a result, they have a huge impact on Zappos's direction and its bottom line. The Zappos core values are:

1. Deliver WOW Through Service
2. Embrace and Drive Change
3. Create Fun and a Little Weirdness
4. Be Adventurous, Creative, and Open-Minded
5. Pursue Growth and Learning
6. Build Open and Honest Relationships with Communication
7. Build a Positive Team and Family Spirit
8. Do More with Less
9. Be Passionate and Determined
10. Be Humble

According to Zappos CEO Tony Hsieh, he and his team wanted to make sure not just that these core values reflected the company's culture, but that employees would actually use them to guide their decision making. Says Hsieh:

> A lot of corporations have "core values" or "guiding principles," but the problem is that they're usually very lofty sounding and they read like a press release that the marketing department put out. A lot of times, an employee might learn about them on day one of orientation, but then the values just end up being part of a meaningless plaque on the wall of the corporate lobby. We wanted to make sure that didn't happen with our core values. We wanted a list of committable core values that we were willing to hire and fire on. If we weren't willing to do that, then they weren't really "values."[1]

When it comes to purpose, Tony Hsieh thinks that Zappos should do at least two things, and do them very well. First, it should be the online service leader, the brand with the very best service. Second, it should create happiness. In fact, Hsieh believes so strongly in this second purpose that he wrote a book and started a company (Delivering Happiness, www.deliveringhappiness.com) to help teach others how to deliver happiness to their employees, customers, vendors, and investors.

Research has found that companies with a higher sense of purpose outperform others by 400 percent. In addition, these companies enjoy:

- 300 percent more innovation
- 44 percent higher retention
- 37 percent increase in sales
- 31 percent increase in productivity
- 125 percent less burnout
- 66 percent fewer sick leaves
- 51 percent less turnover[2]

The Great Place to Work Institute (www.greatplacetowork.com) has been tracking the characteristics and performance of companies that make its list of 100 Best Companies to Work For. From the employees' perspective, a great workplace is one where they:

- Trust the people they work for
- Have pride in what they do
- Enjoy the people they work with

From the managers' perspective, a great workplace is one where:

- They achieve organizational objectives.
- Employees give their personal best.

- They work together as a team or family in an environment of trust.

According to the Great Place to Work Institute, companies on its list perform almost two times better than the general market, and they provide more than twice the return. In addition, employee turnover is significantly lower.[3]

Clearly, values and purpose have a positive impact, both on companies and on employees, customers, vendors, investors, communities, and other organizational stakeholders. Do you know what your company's values and purpose are? Have you stated them clearly and promoted them widely within your organization and among your customers and other stakeholders? Do you and your coworkers, employees, and associates personally live them? If you answered no to any of these questions, then you should take some time to define your company's values and purpose, ideally with the input and active participation of your employees. And once you have your values and purpose figured out, you should make a point of living them.

LIVE YOUR CORE VALUES

In order to succeed as a values-based leader who is committed to balancing a company's profit and self-interest with the common good of its employees and other stakeholders, it is important that you first take the time for self-reflection to determine the core values that will guide your career. These are the values that will both define and differentiate you. When you are determining your values, be mindful of the "permission-to-play" values, the values that sound nice but are the bare minimum. For instance, honesty is a permission-to-play value. Honesty is assumed to be a bare minimum for doing business and having sustainable growth in your career. Determine through self-reflection what differentiates you.

By reflecting on my own career, I have identified that my personal core values are humility, integrity (being honest with myself), and failing gracefully. One of the guiding principles of values-based leadership is the desire to constantly improve. This is the aspiration to lead with your best foot forward and to lift yourself, your team, and your organization up.

In my purse, I keep a printed list of values that are important to me. Depending on your religious persuasion, you can keep a card or two of prayers or meditations. I keep one card for core values and one card for prayers; they are closely related. When you find yourself losing your focus, and all else fails, then step back for a minute or two and center on who you want to be. You may not be able to control your feelings, but you *can* control your actions.

The empowering news is that feelings are built just like anything else. Through controlling your actions, you can influence your feelings. If you remind yourself of the behavior that you hope to show, your impulses and your intuition will follow—you are not bound by anything that is outside your control. There is a strategy for self-improvement. There is a strategy for maintaining emotional health. Remember that the actions you take will affect how you feel. Have patience with yourself. These changes don't happen overnight. Keep the cards on hand to remind yourself of the conscious direction that you want to move in.

Our core values serve as a foundation of our strength. They serve to refocus our heart, mind, and body toward power and ability. Most of us have a general sense of our values, but we may have a difficult time articulating them. Think of how we might be able to help ourselves if we truly understand our own values in depth and focus on those values during the endless stream of decisions that we are faced with every day. Live to be a good example that you are proud of, live to be an example whom you would follow yourself, and strive for self-improvement by holding true to your values. Every day, we have the choice of helping ourselves move forward or taking ourselves backward. Without self-awareness, it is sometimes hard to see how the decisions we are making influence our path in life.

One of my biggest pet peeves is hearing someone say, "I had to," or the idea that somehow, in some way, that person was "made to" perform some action. I advocate having less respect for authority. Usually, there isn't a gun to your head. You must take responsibility for the consequences of your actions. I advocate taking control of all the little things you do each day that you have influence over. We have all heard the idea of turning a problem into an opportunity. You don't need a problem to create an opportunity—all you need is the drive to create an opportunity. Ask yourself, "What can I do in this situation to help myself?"

One of the greatest unsung powers that each of us has is the power to psych ourselves up for success by investing in a firm foundation. When I speak at conferences, I stress the importance of making regular investments in the core values that are truly important to us. By doing so, we are reinforcing within ourselves our unique worth, our gifts, and our credibility. I ask those in my audience to take a few seconds to articulate three core values that are important to them. Once they have articulated and defined these values, I challenge those in my audience to rededicate themselves to being a poster child for those three core values.

By knowing your core values and having them at the forefront of your mind when key decisions present themselves, you have a ready guide for staying true to who you want to be at the end of the day. This removes all those moments of self-doubt, it dials the pressure of expectations way down, and it leaves you firm in the decisions that you've made because you are able to justify why you've made them. This is an excellent way for you to make decisions with confidence and have a life filled with positive achievements.

Your core values do not need to be important to anyone but you. Being present with your family at all times can be a core value. Being a model of maturity at work is a perfectly appropriate core value. Being a person who has an adventurous spirit or one who is fun to work with can be on your short list. The truth is, it doesn't matter what core values you choose; the only thing that matters is that, when you are tested, you know with certainty what you stand for. You can be pushed, but you're practiced at not budging on the issues that mean something to you because you trust your core values. By empowering your core values, you are cultivating your true, authentic voice and your sense of self.

I don't mean to say that you should limit your core values to three. Human beings are complex, so I anticipate that you will have many values. Picking the three that are most important to you provides you with an ethical compass; all the other values keep you balanced.

My personal core values are humility, integrity, and failing gracefully. Let's consider each in turn.

Humility

Humility can mean different things to different people. To me, the phrase that always comes to mind is, "If you are starting to feel like a big fish, you need to reevaluate the size of your pond." Humility acknowledges that there is a higher power or cause: each of us contributes to something that is greater than ourselves. I find hope in the idea that my contributions are part of a larger system.

In my dual careers as an athlete and an engineer, I have seen many talented people brought down because they forgot about humility—they got too big for their britches, and this never ends well. We all struggle with the delicate balance between exuding confidence in order to make a mark, but doing so only to an appropriate degree so that we do not get ahead of our current skill level, experience, and education. It's a tightrope wire that we cross every day.

In 2011, I completed my second IRONMAN with a time of 11:40, and I received a lot of attention for this accomplishment. For the first time in my life, I was seen as an athlete rather than just a participant. For the first time since losing my vision, I thought and felt that I really could make something of this. I was on top of the world! There was a large part of me that felt entirely invincible.

It was only after I leaped to the next level of competition—to the sprint triathlon at the International Triathlon Union—that I quickly learned humility. I was a big fish in a small pond, and jumping into that new bigger pond had created some serious growing pains. I entered my first world championship fully expecting that I could win, regardless of the fact that I had never done a sprint distance triathlon. My triathlon career up to that point had been one half IRONMAN and two full IRONMAN competitions. Sometimes people assume that the shorter-distance triathlons are easier, but in fact they are two different sports. It is like the difference between running a marathon and running a 200-meter dash. It takes hard work to do either, but being good at one doesn't necessarily mean that you will be good at the other.

A saying that I love and repeat often is, "Confidence is the sensation you have right before you are fully aware of your situation." Success in IRONMAN Lake Placid and IRONMAN Texas had boosted my confidence. Immediately after racing in IRONMAN Texas, I became aware of the opportunity to race with the U.S. national team in Beijing, China. The prospect of representing my country on the international stage gave me butterflies in my stomach. I was still so new to the sport of triathlon. In part, I felt that the success I had had up to that point was based on haphazard training and good luck. I had worked hard, but it takes years to cultivate the skills that are needed if you are to excel. I was just barely getting my triathlon legs under me.

That said, I knew that I stood a chance of winning in Beijing. I compared my run times, and they were good. I compared my bike times, and they were encouraging. My swim was slower because I had been swimming for only a year. Thus, I found myself at the starting line of an international race with inflated confidence. I learned the lesson of humility quickly. As a new swimmer, I was still largely hindered by a fear of water. About 200 meters into an 800-meter swim, I had a panic attack. At the exact time that I should have been attacking the swim, I was consumed by fear at a survival level. I feared for my life in a completely irrational way.

Panic attacks aren't reasonable—you can't reason with the unreasonable. My guide was afraid that I wouldn't finish. It was at this moment that I realized that everything was on the line. I realized in quite a literal fashion that I had the choice to sink or swim. I did everything in my power just to move my body through the water. I gave up on good form; I gave up on trying to make it look good. I did some sort of violent dog paddle just to complete the remaining 600 meters.

We finally made it. I knew then with ferocity that we had to make up the time on the bike and on the run. After a humiliating swim, a strong bike, and a powerful run, we finished third, winning bronze for the United States. While I will always be proud of my first international race and proud to have returned with a medal, more than anything else, this experience taught me to have a strong, healthy respect for my peers and for the competition. I overestimated myself and underestimated my peers. This lesson in humility has been with me every instant since.

I knew at that moment exactly what I was capable of, and that I hadn't set myself up for success. I hadn't used strong psychology to position myself for strength. I had entered the race with arrogance as my core value, and it came back to bite me. I had not appropriately respected my competition, and I left feeling humbled. I left knowing that I had not dialed into some magically strong work ethic and that I was not invincible.

I have since learned my lesson, and I recognize that with every new challenge, a person needs to go through the fundamentals. I have humility because I know all the work my competitors have done, the talent that they bring to the table, and all that they have overcome. I hope to bring in a work ethic to match theirs and eventually exceed their results, with reverence for their journey as well.

Integrity

When I use the word *integrity*, people always assume that I mean integrity as seen by the outside world. While I believe that this kind of integrity is extremely important, what I mean here is integrity of the internal variety—integrity within you.

I hear excuses, rationalizations, and justifications daily. Excuses are trip wires that will only get in your way. It sounds like this: "I would have, but . . ." We all make excuses; each of us is masterful at manufacturing excuses. I am no exception. I have slept through swim practice and stayed out too late. Each time, the only one who suffers is me. So if you catch yourself saying, "but . . .," remember that the only person you are underserving is yourself.

No one but you is brought down by a justification. Think of the many times people bring junk food to work. Every day I could say, "I can have a little bit because I had a good workout this morning," but my heart is set on being competitive, and that justification only makes my journey in athletics that much more difficult. That justification has a negative effect on me. I don't mean to say that eating junk food is always off-limits, but I try to be mindful of how the decisions I make influence my journey toward my goals.

A rationalization works along the same lines. A rationalization can take the form of, "I had to compromise, as it was my only option." You very rarely really *have to* do anything. Be mindful and aware of when rationalizations appear in your language.

I hope to set an example as someone who is honest at all times and who lives my life understanding my own strengths and limitations. For some reason, swimming has been my white whale. It requires precision, technique, and a relaxed aggression. I tend to be better at activities that you can force your way through with brute strength; I swim like a boxer. Learning to slow down and focus on having a strong technique has frequently tested my patience. It is when I am swimming that I need the most self-integrity. A bad swim is never someone else's fault, and a discouraging day only means that I need to swim more. Frustration is going to happen, and I am accountable for how I respond and react to those frustrations.

I try to always be respectful of coaches, guides, and fellow competitors and to strive to be my most patient self. It is equally important that I aspire not just to survive the race, but also to be competitive. It is in the water where my mastery of excuses shows its most creative self. I have caught myself faking foot aches, claiming sickness, and even playing the victim. It is an ongoing battle of "Patricia versus Patricia." Every day, I have to remember not to allow myself to lead with an excuse. I am slowly but surely starting to come out ahead and see improvement as a swimmer through the practice of my own core value of integrity. Do not allow your invented excuses to get the better of you.

Failing Gracefully

The core value that I speak of most often is the idea of failing gracefully. Overcoming self-doubt is no small feat. We are all familiar with the fear of failure, rejection, and denial. I choose to be a person who makes an attempt rather than a person who never tries.

Learned helplessness is the idea that if a person is taught that she is not capable, she will come to see herself as not being capable. Ultimately, it's this belief in her inability that will hold her back.

In my youth, the messages I received said loudly and clearly: college isn't for you; sports aren't for you; good things aren't for you. I did not yet have the tools, the technology, the people, and the fuel to help myself. The attempts I made prior to cultivating the fuel ended in failure. I taught myself that I was not capable, and I started to believe these messages. I started to believe that college wasn't for me. I believed that sports weren't for me, and I even believed that good things weren't for me.

I had learned helplessness.

When I was faced with a challenge, I would believe in my heart that it was something that a blind person just couldn't do under any circumstances. Teachers passed me in classes, reinforcing my sense of being less than others. The educational system insisted that I have a free period every day, driving home the message that I couldn't keep up on my own. My attempts to refuse the special treatment were regularly shot down. It was easier for school administrators and teachers to pass me than to make learning accessible to me, so passing became a reasonable accommodation. I'm still saddened today by the reduced expectations placed on me. Even at a young age, I knew that the path I was on was far less than the path I wanted to be on.

It was my strong desire to create a better life for myself that drove me to change the trajectory I was on. It was completely possible that I wouldn't make it, but I still wanted to know for sure. I knew that the only way for me to put that question to rest was to try. So I started my senior year of high school focusing everything on getting into college. I demanded to take the SAT in Braille, which was hard. I focused on my schoolwork while working evenings and weekends at Taco Bell. It was at this point in my life that I started to cultivate a workaholic regimen. I knew that I was behind. I knew that I could prove everyone right. I was driven by my desire to create a better life. Quieting the question "What if?" was enough to propel me forward. After many attempts, I was accepted by a university. I am always grateful for my willingness at a young age to risk failure.

Every day I face fear. Every day I'm afraid of being hurt, injured, or seen as a fool. Every day I remind myself that I'd rather be someone who makes the attempt and risks failure than someone who never tries. Going into the engineering field was a notable attempt at risking failure. I wasn't sure how it was going to go, and I fully expected to fail in my first term at school. It was during this attempt and my close brush with failure that I cultivated humility, integrity, and a willingness to fail. I was able to chip away at my education by focusing on these fundamentals. I hadn't been successful in math after I became blind, so when I registered for calculus, I had a rude awakening. I quickly learned that I was going to have to make some investments in reeducation by withdrawing from calculus and registering for trigonometry instead. Taking a step back allowed me to prepare better for what was to come. Swallowing a little pride certainly hurts, but it is often completely worth the discomfort.

A willingness to fail gracefully is how I got into college. It's how I was able to succeed in engineering. It's how I'm able to pursue my hopes and dreams today.

Imagine for a moment a time when you expressed a hope or a dream to a friend and he shot you down. Now imagine that you are blind and 29 years old, and that you've just told your friend that you are going to leave your engineering job, everything you've worked for, in order to be an athlete in a sport he's never heard of. That was a hard conversation. Now imagine telling your family. "Remember how you all thought that I couldn't be an engineer, then I was an engineer? Remember those steady paychecks I get every month? Well, I'm jumping off a cliff in order to pursue my dreams." That conversation was brutal.

When I announced that I was leaving my job at Microsoft, my friends thought that I had lost my footing, and my family thought that I was certifiable. Regardless, I knew that this was the time to publicly declare my faith and belief in myself. What was the risk? If this didn't work out, I was still educated. I could always come back to full-time traditional employment. But I had a limited window of opportunity to pursue the Paralympics. The clock was ticking, and I wasn't getting any younger. In order to stand a chance at success at this blaze goal, I had to go all in. I bet on myself and risked it all. Time will tell, but I've never looked back. I've never been happier, and between you and me, I've never been more financially secure. Betting on myself was undoubtedly the right move.

BE A SOURCE OF LIGHT

A value that I hold dear and consider to be a close fourth to my core values is the idea of being a source of light. There is enough judgment in the world. We are challenged daily to simply feel good enough. I would rather put my love and energy into building someone up than into tearing her down. I'm competitive both on the racecourse and in the office, and I love opportunities for my skills to shine. But more than anything else, I care about the integrity involved in achieving. I don't want to take the easy way out by cutting someone else down. I want to be someone who is encouraging, loving, and kind to all members of my team.

I hope to exemplify positive leadership by living by example, as this is one of my guiding principles that I articulate often to keep myself on the straight and narrow. You can never go wrong by building someone up, and you should never let a positive attempt or a job well done go unnoticed. Live and demonstrate appreciation for your teammates and coworkers. The relationships you build will pay off in the long term.

BLAZE, FUEL, FIRE, AND CORE VALUES

As a public speaker, my gold standard is to have an impact. You must be authentic and sincere in order to reach people. Telling a compelling story is the easy part. Changing behavior and influencing positive change is a challenge. Each audience is different in its demographics, values, aspirations, and experience. In order to influence positive change, you must have some awareness of what changes would be helpful, what values are held dear, and what focus will meet your unique audience where it is right now.

Blind Ambition as a business has been my opportunity to exercise values-based leadership by demonstrating adherence to my own core values. My blaze goal is to help others achieve their highest-level aspirations. To facilitate this goal, I need to cultivate opportunities to educate using my experience and life lessons. The fuel is securing engagements to coach, speak, and share information, to be a source of encouragement and tools to help others succeed.

Finding success in my blaze goal requires ongoing self-reflection. This reflection helps me honor my core values of integrity, humility, and failing gracefully by doing regular check-ins on my own success. Am I truly living up to my own full potential? Am I truly being the source of encouragement to others that I hope to be? Am I truly demonstrating the respect that all my competitors in athletics and in business deserve? Practice self-reflection daily to catch any divergence from your core values early on.

Your core values are the foundation of your strength. Any split second of divergence undermines your power and strength. You can't move forward or propel yourself toward your goals when you've got the brakes on. After each speech, I record the audience response. I ask myself whether I met them where they were. Did I sufficiently tailor the presentation to my client's needs—both stated and unstated? I take notes on ways I can improve my presentations to help those in my audience achieve their goals for the event.

I am better able to cultivate new opportunities for myself as a speaker by prioritizing the values of others. With every engagement, I want those in my audience to leave feeling as if their achievement is my highest priority. I want them to leave feeling that the work they do every day is important to me. I want to offer values-based leadership by balancing my investment in my own core values with my respect for their investment in theirs.

Adherence to my own core values positions me to be strong in the pursuit of my blaze goal of delivering high-impact presentations that are intended to motivate and educate people by providing them with tools and skills that they can start using today to achieve their highest potential. A regular habit of self-reflection supports me in my fuel, fire, blaze goals by giving me opportunities to make corrections whenever they are required. Constantly iterating on improvements makes me an ever-stronger leader, as I am removing any unnecessary resistance to the delivery of my hopes for others' success.

••• LESSONS •••

- It's not enough to have values—you have to live your values and model them to those around you.
- Keep a list of your core values in your pocket, purse, or wallet and refer to it whenever you have to make an important decision.
- Practice self-reflection every day. When you find examples of divergence from your core values, identify opportunities to correct them in the future.

- Try to find an employer or company whose core values and purpose are aligned with your own—and that enables you to live yours every day.
- Live your values and your purpose. Be an example for others in your professional and personal lives.

CHAPTER 9

BE RESILIENT

• • • • • • • • • • • • • • •

ADVERSITY HAS THE EFFECT OF
ELICITING TALENTS WHICH IN
PROSPEROUS CIRCUMSTANCES
WOULD HAVE LAIN DORMANT.

—Horace

What would have to happen for each of us to be assured that we weren't going to be pushed anymore? For each of us to feel that we've been challenged for the last time—that we have no more obstacles in our path? As far as I know, as long as we are living, we will continue to be pushed, face challenges, and find obstacles in our path—and we will need to be *resilient*, ready to bounce back and keep on fighting. The good news is that ours is an inherently resilient species. No matter what adversities, challenges, or obstacles we may face, most of us will do whatever it takes to go over, under, around, or through them. And it's in the darkest of times—the times that we are overwhelmed by the odds and it looks as if we are going to be defeated—that we often shine our brightest.

I thought I had cornered the market on resilience—I thought I knew all about it. I went to engineering college as a blind person, after all; what could be more resilient? I had no support network and I thrived, which in turn enabled me to create a support network; what could be more resilient?

I learned that our opportunities to be resilient are boundless and our capacity to rise to the occasion is equally limitless. It's up to us when, where, and how we will meet the challenges that stand between us and our goals.

THE NATURE OF RESILIENCE (AND HOW TO BUILD IT)

If you think resilience is something that people are born with and either have or don't have, you are wrong. According to the American Psychological Association, building resilience is an ongoing process—it takes time, and it takes effort. In other words, the ability to be resilient can be taught, and it can be learned. And when the people in an organization are resilient—able to recover quickly from setbacks and willing to get back into the fight—their organization will also be resilient.

Participants in a seminar organized for the European Foundation for the Improvement of Living and Working Conditions explored the nature of resilience. During the course of discussions about a number of case studies of businesses that had exhibited the ability to be resilient, the group defined business resilience as:

- the ability of an organization to rebound and learn from adversity;
- the ability to achieve the organization's aspirations regardless of circumstances, with the aim of creating long-term sustainable assets, based on the diverse skills set defined by the people concerned and the competencies involved in the process;
- a continuous process that operates and adapts to achieve best practice while maintaining competitiveness, to refine the offer (stakeholder value), and preserve values in the long term;
- the ability of an organization to adhere to the best they know (excellence and quality), while committing to everything that improves the best they now know (permanent transformation and learning).[1]

While organizations—and the people within them—have always faced adversity and challenges that tested their resilience, the increased velocity of change in the business world requires businesses to be more resilient than ever before. This is pushed to the extreme when unexpected events, such as the crash of a major computer system or a natural disaster, test a company's mettle. Companies that are resilient have a strong competitive advantage over companies that are not.

An inability to respond to business challenges or disruptions can have a distinctly negative impact. According to an IBM report on business resilience,

> When day-to-day business is disrupted, for any reason, the financial impact can ruin your business. The

indirect impacts of downtime such as lost market share, decreased productivity, regulatory non-compliance and damaged reputation are equally damaging.[2]

If your resilience muscles need a workout, what can you do to strengthen them? According to DiscoveryHealth.com, there are 10 ways that anyone can build resilience in himself, including:

- *Make connections.* The old saying, "No man is an island," is true. When it comes to taking on challenges and bouncing back from adversity, there's comfort (and support, and expertise, and willpower, and strength) in numbers. To build resilience, build strong connections with coworkers, colleagues, friends, family, and others. If you aren't making enough connections with others, then consider attending after-work networking groups, joining community-based organizations, or taking part in other activities that will introduce you to new people.
- *Avoid seeing crises as insurmountable problems.* There is no crisis that can't be addressed, dealt with, and solved with the application of sufficient brainpower, expertise, time, and money. And in the case of a problem that is too expensive to solve, or that would take too much time or require resources that you just don't have, then chances are there are plenty of alternatives you can try to go around, over, or under it.
- *Accept that change is a part of living.* Yes, I know that "change happens" is very much a cliché, but many people still think that you can fight change, dramatically slow it down, or perhaps even stop it in its tracks. If that sounds

like you, then what needs to change is your attitude. Everything changes, and the sooner you accept that fact—and modify your behavior accordingly—the sooner you'll build the resilience you need to take on fast-changing business environments and markets.

- *Move toward your goals.* When you start moving toward your goals, you create small successes along the way that build momentum that will carry you through the adversity you face. Instead of worrying about all the things that you can't get done, pick out one or two things that you can get done—and then do them. Any movement toward your goals is a positive thing, and you should make a point of working on and accomplishing at least one thing every day.

- *Take decisive actions.* It's hard to bounce back from adversity when you're wishy-washy in your decisions. If you're always thinking to yourself, "Should I or shouldn't I?," and then changing your mind multiple times after you make an initial, tentative decision—or just hoping that the situation will go away—then you will be hard-pressed to ever achieve your goals. Problems can't be solved if you aren't decisive, and they often don't go away when you ignore them. Sometimes they get worse. So be decisive, and take definite actions.

- *Look for opportunities for self-discovery.* Adversity often brings out the best in us, and we should be on the lookout for personal growth that we may experience as a result of the challenges we face. We are changed by our environment—often in positive ways that add to our capacity to overcome obstacles while building our resilience. Don't assume that you're the same person today as you were five years, five months, or even five days ago. Chances are, you're not.

- *Nurture a positive view of yourself.* There's a reason why your company hired you—because you are a talented person who has skills and knows how to get things done. Think about it for a moment. Would your boss have hired someone who can't deal with the challenges that we all face every day on the job? No, probably not—that would be an incredible waste of time and money, something that no company today can afford to lose. Build positivity within yourself, and push negativity out. You are talented, and you can defeat the problems that are arrayed before you. Now go get 'em!

- *Keep things in perspective.* Yes, things may look bad at the moment—even *very* bad. And they might in fact *be* very bad—again, at the moment. If you stay cool, calm, and collected and keep negative events in perspective, you'll find that you aren't ruled by them. This allows you to build the resilience you'll need to carry you through the inevitable challenges that we all face.

- *Maintain a hopeful outlook.* Believe it or not, things *will* eventually get better. And if you maintain a positive outlook on your business, your career, and your life, then chances are that not only will things get better, but they will get better much sooner than if your outlook is negative.

- *Take care of yourself.* If you're burned out on the job, not getting enough sleep or exercise, or otherwise not taking good care of yourself, then you can be sapping the wellspring of your resilience, leaving you defenseless when adversity strikes. When you take care of yourself by getting plenty of rest, exercising, eating well, and avoiding dependency on drugs and alcohol, you naturally build resilience, and this resilience will really come in handy when the challenges are coming at you fast and furiously.[3]

WE ALL HAVE PROBLEMS

In April 2014, I traveled to Sault Sainte Marie, Michigan, to help my dad, whose health was failing. As adults, we are never really ready for the prospect of losing our parents. It doesn't matter whether you have a broken relationship or one that looks as if it came out of a Norman Rockwell painting; all of that is moot compared to the biological want and need for our parents to be around. Dad and I have a fine relationship, and we have generally always been close. Our greatest challenge is in the incompatibility of our outlooks.

Once when I was in a car with Dad, I told him that I'd give him $5 if he could go 60 seconds without saying something negative. He could say something positive, or neutral, or remain quiet—just nothing negative. His response was, "I don't need your money." That is Dad's quintessential outlook on life. He is a negative person. I am very positive, which is what leads us to butt heads from time to time. All that aside, I hope to see him live a long life. Learning of my dad's failing health rocked my world—I was saddened to the core. I rushed to Michigan to get a better picture from the doctors and to help him in whatever way I could.

I was occupied with cleaning Dad's house when I received a phone call from a number I didn't recognize. It was a neighbor of mine from Austin, Texas. She said, "No need to worry; I've got your dog."

I thought that was strange. I had friends coming by to let Camilla out, so why in the world would my neighbor have her? So I asked, "Oh, did she get out?"

My neighbor said, "No, your apartment is on fire. The fire department rescued her."

I had started the week in emotional disarray because of my father's failing health, only to discover that my bad situation had just gotten worse. I had lost everything, and on top of that, I couldn't get home. There aren't many flights from Sault Sainte Marie to Austin. I was a nervous wreck.

I am a public speaker who presents on the topic of resilience, and here I was being forced to be more resilient than ever. I was terrified and saddened. All my friends offered to help in whatever way they could, but I had no idea how they could help me. People kept offering to help me move. I kept thinking, "I have one suitcase half-packed. I could move on the bus. I have nothing." Of course I appreciated the sentiment, but I had no idea what to say in response.

I felt as if I had just been thrown out of a plane without a parachute. Like the good engineer that I am, I tried my best to reason my way through it. My dad is uncomfortable with expressions of emotion. While I was in public view, I kept calm and took a stab at problem solving, but in the privacy of my hotel room, I crumbled. I cried uncontrollably. I had no idea what to do. I had many friends who offered me a place to stay for as long as I needed, but that felt like a Band-Aid on the fact that I couldn't go home. I felt helpless.

I decided to adopt a coping mechanism of continuing with my routine and occupying my mind in whatever way was possible. Getting through a situation like that requires a lot of hurry up and wait. I returned from Michigan early, leaving Dad to fend for himself. I felt awful abandoning him in his time of need. There is no correct plural for emergency.

I made it home. I stayed with friends with my suitcase of winter clothes, which were useless in Austin. I immediately called an apartment locator service and set my mind to finding a new home. Mine was completely destroyed, so there was no hope of moving back in.

I returned to work at Mozido a few days later. I wanted to be invisible. I was hoping that no one would notice me. I felt broken—broken like I couldn't put together even one sentence. I told my boss that I couldn't find a silver lining, no matter how desperately I tried. I felt that I had passed a breaking point.

That day at lunch, there was a strange meeting with an ambiguous title on our schedule: "Strategy planning event, pizza provided." I didn't think anything of it. My plan was to hug the back wall and keep my mouth shut.

When everyone arrived at the meeting, I was called to the front of the room. I was shaking because I so desperately wanted to be invisible. My boss and my coworkers had raised $3,600 to help me get through my difficult time. I broke down crying in front of all of them. I was speechless. I held on as long as I could before ducking into the stairwell, where I collapsed and cried. The money was enough to replace everything, but more than that, what meant so much to me was feeling a sense of belonging. I was devastated, and they all cared enough about me to help me. It is one thing to talk about helping, but each one of them had actually contributed; their actions spoke volumes.

Prior to their kindness, I had never been so low. I honestly think that that week, when I lost my home while preparing to lose a parent, was harder on me than losing my vision. I felt broken, but my coworkers' gesture helped me feel less broken, and with their sincere friendship, I was able to turn the corner. It was with their help that I was able to get back on my feet in exactly two weeks.

We all need support networks; without them, we are alone in the world. Invest in your support network by consistently, predictably being the person you want to be. When I desperately needed help, when I had no idea what to ask for, I didn't have to ask. When my own capacity to be resilient was stretched to the breaking point, my support network helped relieve the tension. My support network of coworkers, friends, and family members came through better than any insurance policy ever could have.

I found an apartment. Two weeks to the day after the fateful call from my neighbor, the broken pieces of my life were all back in place.

Throughout the entire experience, I missed just one day of workouts. While I will always be sad at having felt displaced and having faced a vicious attack on my sense of security, I will always be grateful that I saw firsthand how many people are invested in seeing me succeed. I had grown up feeling that my efforts would be an exercise in failure, but in my lowest moment, the only message that came through loud and clear was, "We won't let you fail." I grew up feeling that I had no lifeline, but in my time of need, I felt that I had an army I didn't even know about. I left that sad situation feeling only blessed and loved, and thankful to be alive.

Resilience is a key factor in obtaining and maintaining credibility in the workforce, a positive trajectory toward our goals, and our ability to cultivate well-being and balance. That having been said, life is hard—even when your life is filled with good things. There is so much push and pull in our daily lives. It is our capacity for resilience that enables each of us to thrive. Resilience is the glue of our emotional and mental health that allows each of us to bounce back and resume our former shape, and the toolkit that we always carry with us for recovering from the challenges and adversity that are inevitable.

I love the Horace quotation that opens this chapter. It explains that we need to be challenged by adversity if we are to demonstrate our full potential. What would we learn about ourselves if we were never challenged? If I met someone who had never experienced some adversity, I'm not sure I'd trust that person. Being challenged can be painful, but it is good for each of us because it gives us the opportunity to cultivate new skills—and to show a level of resilience that we didn't know we had within us.

INTERRUPTIONS

To do our best work, some amount of focused effort is required, but it is often very difficult to find opportunities to focus when e-mails, texts, phone calls, and social media updates—along with the daily demands of coworkers, family, and friends—interrupt our concentration and vie for our attention at every step. Managing interruptions requires some resilience because they invoke an emotional response of frustration and even disappointment if we are unable to get as much done as we had hoped, and because we must rebound from the interruptions and quickly get back on task.

My response to interruptions is twofold.

First, discover the hours when you work best. It might be in the morning after your children go to school, or it could be late at night after everyone else is in bed. It takes only an hour of focused effort to launch yourself forward. I tend to work best early in the morning after my first workout, so I block off the time from 8:00

to 9:30 in the morning to get the bulk of my work done for the day. Since I have started this practice, I have noticed a dramatic drop in my frustration with interruptions.

The second component is to communicate to friends, family, and coworkers that this hour that you have set aside every day is *your* time. This is not foolproof; inevitably there will still be occasions when people feel it is necessary to interrupt you with something. But in communicating your strategy, you are creating the opportunity for others to respect your wish for a focused effort.

SOCIAL CONFLICTS

Truth be told, I don't like every single person that I come in contact with, and I'm sure not everyone likes me. In the corporate world, we call this "different working styles," but at the end of the day, we are all human beings. There are some people with whom we work seamlessly and communicate with ease, and then there are others with whom we do not. Social conflicts in the workplace can leave us feeling attacked, annoyed, or even aggressive. It is in these situations that we are presented with countless opportunities to make a career-limiting move.

In the face of social conflicts, we must muster our better selves to demonstrate high resilience. Try to begin each day with the authentic hope that you will find common ground with the particular individual with whom you are struggling. It also helps to write a list of two or three common incentives. For example, if I have a coworker who is fighting for the same resources as I am, it is key for me to remind myself that we are both working hard to move the same company forward. It is important that you try to be patient. Patience is not mythical—it is a virtue that can be cultivated with practice and dedication. Patience comes with training, just like any other skill.

PILES OF WORK

Most of us have more work than we can realistically complete, and this leaves us feeling perpetually behind. But guess what? This is yet another opportunity to demonstrate resilience. I know that when the piles of work are growing before my eyes, my tendency is to want to throw up my hands and walk out. When reaching the bottom of the pile seems unattainable, I have learned that the hardest part is just getting started.

So when the piles of work are starting to grow sky-high, I set a goal of dedicating an additional 30 minutes to focused effort. Even if I get only 30 minutes, I find that I've made a dent, and more often than not, I end up dedicating more than the original 30 minutes to the task. When things are piling up, I also have found it beneficial to do the opposite and invest some time in developing a new efficiency practice. It is in these times of constrained resources that I invest in learning new tools like mental mapping, organizational strategy, brainstorming techniques, or other creative ways to get more work done in a shorter amount of time.

Try either approach—or both—and see how they work for you.

CONFLICTING PRIORITIES

Imagine this scenario: you have ten things to get done, and all of them are your highest priority—a situation that we all face daily. At that point, priority is meaningless. It is in these situations that we need to understand the impact of stress on our ability to function.

Feeling bogged down will only discourage you, but it is in these moments that you need a win. To begin prioritizing, first pick the easiest task to finish and complete it. Then pick the next easiest task, and keep moving forward toward the tasks that are more difficult to complete.

If this strategy doesn't work for you, figure out which items can benefit from collaboration or which items can be done in parallel. Ask yourself, "What can I get done and off my plate in the next hour?" Do everything you can to start chipping away at your list. If the priorities are truly conflicting, reevaluate them and make sure you have a strategy that is helping you move forward. Evaluate the conflicts against your fuel, fire, blaze goals to ensure that each item brings you closer to your personal end game.

MANAGING DEPENDENCIES

Collaboration can be a beautiful thing that leads us to new and more creative solutions. It can improve our enjoyment of our work by providing us with opportunities to cultivate working relationships and make our everyday interactions unique and interesting. Collaboration can also introduce dependencies that challenge us by forcing us to accommodate someone else's schedule and incorporate someone else's deadlines into our own schedules and deadlines.

None of us has the capacity to control everything in our projects and deliverables. Sometimes managing dependencies can make us feel that we are doing someone else's job. This is another opportunity to demonstrate high resilience as we adapt and find more creative solutions for communicating challenges and planning for a successful collaboration. It is in the face of managing dependencies that we need to not only practice patience, but also practice empathy by trying to understand our colleague's concerns. We need to lead with the assumption that we have a common goal, but that there may be factors affecting this coworker that we may not be aware of. Resilience in managing dependencies is rooted in trust that all involved parties have the best intentions, common goals, and a vested interest in mutual success.

Our opportunities to demonstrate resilience are abundant and boundless. My challenge for you is to think about a few opportunities you have to differentiate yourself from others by demonstrating high resilience. Think of three of these opportunities, then detail one behavior that you can change today to begin the progressive cultivation of a positive habit. Keep in mind that it takes 21 days of consistent practice to cultivate a positive habit. If you practice your new behavior every day, it will become second nature, and you will be that much closer to thriving with a higher level of resilience.

I practice resilience daily to conquer the cultural misperceptions of a person with blindness. The world doesn't expect a lot from me, and people are shocked to find that I am competent and successful. These assumptions hurt me every time, and when I feel the need to prove myself, I remind myself to practice emotional vulnerability. To change my reaction to cultural misperceptions, I must change my response to that hurt—the worst possible reaction being defensiveness. In those moments, I can choose to respond with a thoughtful explanation, or decide that it simply isn't worth it to me and move on.

COMMUNICATING MY DIVERSE NEEDS

Every blind person you will ever meet is going to have different needs. I desperately need to be treated as an equal—to have those who work with me on a regular basis act normal. I don't need a narration of images; I don't need to be called out as different. I just need to be treated as a contributing member of the workforce who is held to the same high, if not higher, standards.

In order to accomplish this, I communicate my hopes and ambitions to my coworkers so that they know that my intent in the workforce is not to participate, but to lead—I say in spite of my disability, but what I really mean to say is, in spite of any challenges that I may encounter. I intend to demonstrate high resilience always and, in doing so, position myself for ongoing success.

TAKING ON THE RIGHT AMOUNT OF WORK

I feel a need to prove my value every day. I am working hard to better understand that challenges are not unique to me and that my value is self-evident in the quality of my work. My tendency to be a workaholic and an overachiever is sustainable only until something happens to disturb my work-life balance. By quieting the overachiever in me and taking on only the amount of work that I know with certainty I can do well, I am demonstrating high resilience.

To establish value, I have to be willing to change a behavior. I always want to be the first to volunteer and to be the one who is perceived as being more capable than others, but taking on more than I realistically can handle would only prove that I am limited. I strive to set myself up for success by carefully picking and choosing commitments that I can keep, with a tiny bit of slack in the schedule to accommodate the unpredictability of real life.

Resilience is a word that is thrown around so often that it can lose its meaning. Take this opportunity to redefine what resilience means to you. Have some respect for the challenges you face, and devise a plan for tackling them so that you can begin to cultivate a habit of resilience. Remember that we are blessed with adversity because it provides each of us with the opportunity to demonstrate talents that we might otherwise never have had the chance to express.

PUTTING RESILIENCE TO WORK

When I decided to leave Microsoft to start Blind Ambition, I knew that I was jumping off a cliff. When I gave my exit interview, I was so excited about my new career that I almost took my HR rep with me. Anyone who has made the transition from a comfortable job with outstanding benefits to the rocky lifestyle of self-employment can understand that the challenges I would face differed greatly from the challenges I anticipated. My greatest fear was the loss of income and being unable to pay my basic bills. In fact, the money came easily. The true problem was energy.

Initially, I had planned to develop one stock speech and make minor alterations to it, depending on the audience. I successfully delivered this one speech for two months before I was bored out of my mind. I quickly realized that this new career of mine would be short-lived if I didn't keep my presentations fresh with new life lessons and content that audiences could relate to. I increased my rate and planned for a minimum of 10 hours of preparation to write a fresh speech for each client and rehearse it.

When you work for yourself, you set your own value. Setting a higher value for my speaking services felt like jumping off yet another cliff. Increasing the quality while reducing the quantity was my opportunity to demonstrate resilience. The first few months were unsustainable; I was traveling all over the country, making little money and having no energy left to train. I quickly saw that I was on a sure path to failure. For this venture to be a success, I had to reframe my business and my product to ensure authenticity and sincerity with my audiences. To safeguard my ability to be resilient, I would have to carve out some time for close relationships and rest to maintain a positive view and outlook.

While I was now much happier with my content, I found myself overworked. When I factored in the time it took to travel to client sites, it was hard to find the time to train. If I was unable to train, both my career as a speaker and my ability to remain competitive in my sport would be compromised. Neither of these outcomes was acceptable to me.

Giving a stock speech left my content flat. I had heard it too many times. Writing fresh speeches took much more energy, but the speeches were better. I determined that if this venture was to be sustainable and successful, I was going to need to guard my emotional energy as a precious resource. I knew that something had to give. I needed to get in front of bigger audiences in order to do fewer speeches. I would move to a boutique offering with less volume. I determined to engage with some of the bigger speaking bureaus for bookings and set the bar high for my rate.

My blaze goal was to help others achieve their highest ambitions by learning from my experience, failures, and successes. My fire was securing audiences and offering an engaging service with sincerity and authenticity. My fuel was keeping my experiences fresh, maintaining my emotional health, and customizing my day-to-day offerings.

Leaving the security of my job at Microsoft and taking the leap to self-employment wasn't easy, but I did it. In doing this, I have had numerous opportunities to exercise my resilience. And while my resilience muscles have always been in pretty good shape, the more I exercise them, the stronger they get. At this point, I honestly feel that there's no disaster from which I cannot recover, no crisis that I cannot overcome. I have been tested over and over again, and I keep bouncing back.

What adversities do you face on an occasional or ongoing basis? How do you deal with them? Have you enlisted a network of coworkers, friends, and family members to help you through them? Take every opportunity you can to build your own resilience muscles. You'll find that the more you cultivate the ability to bounce back from adversity, the deeper your capacity to face it will be.

··· LESSONS ···

- Build your own resilience by making connections, seeing crises as solvable, accepting change, moving toward your goals, taking decisive action, engaging in self-discovery, having a positive self-image, keeping things in perspective, being hopeful, and taking good care of yourself.
- Multitasking is a myth. Trying to do too much at once can result in lower performance. Minimize the distractions in your work environment, and focus your full attention on one task at a time.
- Demonstrate your resilience in personal relationships by finding common ground with others in the event of disagreements. Build on this common ground to reach agreement. Exercise patience, and you will be rewarded.

- When the work is piling up, devote an extended period of time to clearing out the backlog. Invest in learning new tools that can make you more effective and efficient in your job.
- Prioritize your work—and work your priorities. Doing so will help you avert the disasters that can push you to your limits.
- Don't take on more work than you can realistically accomplish. You will deplete your reserve of resilience, leaving you ill equipped when you really need it.

CHAPTER 10

BUILD WILLPOWER AND GOAL-CENTRIC HABITS

· · · · · · · · · · · · · · ·

WE ARE WHAT WE REPEATEDLY DO.
EXCELLENCE, THEN, IS NOT AN ACT,
BUT A HABIT.

—Aristotle

Willpower is not something that you are born with—it is something that you develop. It is the ability to put the requirements of your long-term goals above immediate gratification. Willpower is always being aware of the consequences of all your decisions, both big and small. According to research conducted by psychologist Martin Seligman, self-discipline—or willpower—is a greater predictor of long-term success than is IQ.

At all those times when I felt I was outclassed in school, I have been able to overcome that sense of self-doubt by reminding myself that, although I am not a naturally gifted person, I do have a great deal of willpower. I have learned that with willpower and self-discipline, I can be successful and challenge anyone—anyplace, anytime. But I also know that my willpower can slip away if exercising it doesn't become an everyday habit.

SELF-CONTROL, WILLPOWER, AND FORCE OF HABIT

According to the American Psychological Association, people who have self-control and willpower often experience a variety of positive results, including better mental and physical health, better finances, increased self-esteem, lower rates of substance abuse, and better grades in school. Some social scientists compare willpower to a muscle. It can be strengthened, but it can also be fatigued through overuse, which is known as *willpower depletion*. According to researchers at the University of Toronto, the activity in the part of the brain that is correlated with cognition—the anterior cingulate cortex—is markedly decreased in people whose willpower is depleted by tasks that require self-control.[1]

Cultivating healthy habits can strengthen our willpower by creating defaults in our decision-making process to make positive decision making automatic, thus reducing the load on our willpower muscle. Reducing willpower muscle fatigue helps people make repeated positive decisions over time.

In a world that is full of tempting food, distractions, and plug-and-play excuses, we all face an ongoing struggle to maintain our physical, emotional, and mental well-being. The struggle exists at the decision point—we feel that we deserve a treat in return for all our good decisions, but the truth is, every time we give in to our desire for a treat or a reward, we make the next healthy decision even harder for ourselves. By removing the option—and the resulting struggle—we are saving ourselves from willpower fatigue and exhaustion and cultivating a healthy pattern.

According to the American Psychological Association's annual Stress in America survey, 27 percent of Americans point to their lack of willpower in following through as their number one barrier to change. However, a clear majority of survey respondents were optimistic on the topic, reporting that they believed that willpower is not just something that one is born with, but that it can be learned.[2] Willpower is a skill that you develop through purposeful effort.

Roy Baumeister at Florida State University is one of the leading researchers on willpower and positive change. His research indicates that in influencing positive change in your life, three factors come into play.

The first factor is establishing motivation. This is accomplished using the fuel, fire, blaze hierarchy presented in this book. Link your blaze goal, with your highest-level emotional intrinsic motivation, to your fuel goals, your day-to-day habits and behaviors.

The second factor is monitoring your behavior relative to that goal. Choose one or two behaviors that support your blaze goal and embark on a 21-day experiment to practice those behaviors. Depending on the behavior, it may help to have realistic affirming checkpoints along the way—if the checks are unrealistic, you will only undermine yourself. For example, if your goal is to get promoted within one week—something that might normally take a year or more to achieve—you may feel defeated when you have not been successful seven days later. Set yourself up for long-term success by using realistic checkpoints that are intended to make you feel and see improvement as a result of your hard work.

The third factor—and the finishing piece—is the development of willpower by implementing positive changes in your life. Willpower is developed through conscientious decision making, mindfulness of healthy patterns, and a heartfelt desire to make your own life easier. Mark Muraven, PhD, and his research team at the University at Albany discovered that the people who were most easily depleted of willpower were those same people who felt compelled to exert self-control—much more so than people who were motivated by their internal goals and desires. "When it comes to willpower, those who are in touch with themselves may be better off than their people-pleasing counterparts," he wrote.[3]

Creating a healthy habit takes discipline up front, but the advantage is that by making the behavior a natural response, you are removing the requirement for ongoing discipline—you are positioning yourself for long-term success by developing positive reflexes that help you reach your goals. I read in an article that one of the things that sets Olympic athletes apart from the rest of us is their capacity for boredom. So much of excelling in a sport is making tiny adjustments and perfecting the way you move. This requires countless hours of practicing form, technique, and repetitive movements until they feel natural.

Creating healthy habits is very similar to developing muscle memory—once muscle memory, or the healthy habit, is perfected, you remove the decision process. It is like unleashing the power of your own autopilot to make the healthy decision a reflex. The good news is that this autopilot is within your control. With purpose, practice, and persistence, you can make moving toward your goals a natural reflex.

Bad habits will make you work harder, and they will only take you farther from your goals. The good news is that creating good habits and bad habits requires roughly equivalent amounts of effort. It takes approximately 21 days to create a habit, whether it's a good one or a bad one. Remember:

- It is within your power to create a positive habit.
- It is within your power to stop a bad habit before it becomes a problem.
- Putting some thought into the habits you want to create and treating habits as a means to conserve your energy can empower you.

HOW TO MAKE PURPOSEFUL HABITS

First and foremost, if habits are to be effective, they have to support your goals. Review your fuel, fire, blaze goals and determine a few behaviors that will help push you toward your blaze goals. The key here is not to overwhelm yourself—pick just two or three behaviors that you want to change right away, then take a minute to write a few sentences to answer the following questions: How will this help me? What do I need to do? When should I see results? Clearly determine the results that you hope to obtain, and do your best to answer the questions as realistically as possible given the information you have at hand.

Once you have really developed the purpose, intent, and execution for your goals, you then need to commit to doing the new behavior for 21 days—this is enough time to make it automatic. Don't worry if you miss a day. Remember, this is an exercise in self-improvement, not in cultivating perfection. Be forgiving if you slip up, and be appreciative of the times when you do follow through with your new habit. Positive reinforcement in and of itself is effective. Remember to applaud the successes of your own new positive behaviors.

While I was dealing with the simultaneous crises of my dad's failing health and losing my apartment, I decided that the habit I wanted to create was to cultivate my support system. I was in the throes of a crash course in emotional vulnerability, and I felt broken. I determined that my coping mechanism for the next 21 days would be to express appreciation for my friends and family.

What Do I Need to Do?

With regard to the actual behavior, do your best to keep it simple. In the case of responding to my supporters, I sent one piece of communication to my network each day with a sincere sentiment of appreciation: a text, e-mail, phone call—something quick and easy to express the depth of my appreciation. These new behaviors don't need to move mountains. You should feel free to start small with achievable daily goals. Mountains move over time, so begin with what is within your control today.

When Should I See Results?

In my case, I was expecting immediate results from expressing gratitude to my friends and family. My goal was to deepen my connections and also improve my own outlook by investing in my foundation. In my lowest moments, the coping mechanism of being free with thank yous has left me feeling that I'm not a helpless victim—I still have some say in cultivating a positive outlook.

One key to cultivating a positive habit is consistency and follow-through. I set reminders on my phone for 21 days. I had to perform the behavior before I could dismiss the reminder. I have been supported by so many people that when I see the reminder, sending out words of gratitude via whatever communication means are available to me at that moment has become natural. For other plan-intensive behaviors, the reminder may need to be timed. For example, if your intent is to practice a specific exercise, you may need to plan that reminder the night before or two hours before in order to prepare the right food, clothes, or transportation required for success.

I thrive on routine, and I prefer to go to the gym at the same time every day and to eat roughly the same food. The key to my success is consistency and a healthy capacity for boredom. If you need variety in your day so that you're not bored to death with the same routine, then cultivate a trigger that means something to you. For example, if you intend to start an exercise regimen and you begin to feel the urge to graze in the kitchen or do some mindless task, go for a quick jog instead—jog as the mood strikes you. Before you know it, whatever trigger you've chosen, whether it's jogging or hula hooping, will naturally lead to your new behavior. This will piggyback onto things you are already doing in order to influence your future behaviors.

Never underestimate the power of support in forming new habits. If a habit is of particular importance to you and you can recruit a friend to join you, then do so. Recruit someone to form a healthy-habit buddy system—we tend to behave in a certain way when we're around those we associate with. Always try to surround yourself with people who exemplify the behaviors that you hope to incorporate or who have the same investment in their self-improvement. Surrounding yourself with people with common aspirations will increase your likelihood of success.

Don't be afraid to replace bad habits with good habits. For example, if your goal is to stop a behavior, such as spending excessive amounts of time surfing the Internet at work, you could commit to walking every time you feel the urge to get lost in your computer—replace the negative behavior with a positive behavior.

Comfort eating is an ongoing struggle for me—when my heart is aching or I feel stressed, I don't necessarily reach for junk food, but I do have a hard time stopping myself from eating. I tend to eat ridiculous quantities of food. Regardless of the fact that I usually grab something healthy, quantity does matter. More than anything, I care that the behavior of comfort eating is masking unrest. I'd rather have a different habit for dealing with distress than stuffing my mouth. Now when I feel the impulse to fill the void with mindless eating, I leave the phone at home, unplug, and walk my dog. I find that this is the perfect way to ground myself and release all that negative emotion.

It's a common belief among most people that acting stoic and in control is a strength. In truth, suppression of our emotional vulnerability and natural reactions only depletes our willpower. Creating a positive pattern of emotional expression and healthy vulnerability can help eliminate the unhealthy habits that we are struggling with. I am known for always being calm, no matter what the circumstances. I once received the following feedback on an annual review, "We used to think that Patricia didn't understand what was happening; we then realized that she is just a calm person." I appreciate my ability to be steady, but learning to express emotional vulnerability to help me deal with my root issues in an effort to conserve my reserves of willpower has been an ongoing struggle.

I mindfully and regularly make a goal of expressing myself in healthy ways so that I can better cope with the trials of life and break unhealthy patterns. Emotional vulnerability is a work in progress. I have learned that in suppressing your emotional reaction, not only are you setting yourself up for willpower exhaustion, but you are forgoing an opportunity to develop deeper relationships.

Negative motivation never pays off. When you are cultivating muscle memory and good routines, remember that your goal is to lift yourself up. Motivation that is rooted in feelings of guilt or unworthiness will only leave you flat. Remember that these changes you are working so hard for will benefit you and your loved ones as you move toward your goals. Do this for yourself, and do it for those you love. Abandon the guilt and negativity and celebrate your successes. As soon as you start to see the benefits, share your triumphs with someone you are close to, write it down, or do whatever it takes to remind yourself of the progress you are seeing.

Habits can be our greatest asset or our greatest detriment. The good news is that our habits begin with a choice. Remember that every action we take sets a precedent for future actions, and that every positive action reinforces a pattern of healthy activities. In turn, negative behavior begets more negative decisions.

My dad has an expression that I've always enjoyed: "I've taken the wrong turn so many times that now the wrong turn looks so familiar that I end up taking it again." We will operate the way we have practiced, and we will adapt to the environment we create for ourselves. Creating healthy patterns and habits is our responsibility. Every habit is an answer to the questions, "How will I behave?," "Who will I invite into my community?," and "What are my goals, and how committed am I to reaching my goals?" These choices should be made with intent and purpose, always cognizant of your fuel, fire, blaze goals. Cultivate your habits carefully so that they fan the fire of your blaze goals.

Habits at Work

When I first started working at Microsoft, my organizational habits were abysmal. I had never used a calendar for productivity—I had no system for organizing time or any understanding of useful communication. This was a problem because my employment at Microsoft came with the heaviest workload I had ever had to deal with. I quickly understood that I needed to do something to help myself get organized and ahead of my work instead of being constantly behind it. I did not immediately know whether doing so would help me stay on top of my demanding workload, but I certainly hoped that it would.

At lunch, my coworkers would compare notes on productivity articles they had read and the strategies they used to manage their time. I thought these were the most boring topics imaginable. It took about a month for me to understand that their openness to productivity advice was exactly what I needed. I was behind not because of my vision, but because I had not been open to helping myself. There were tools all around me—I just had to learn to use them.

I became an avid follower of several business publications and read everything I could get my hands on that explored the positive habits that I could adopt to get better organized and help myself. After filling my toolbox with a new set of healthy habits gleaned from these publications—and from many conversations with my coworkers—I was able not only to keep up, but to excel among an able-bodied field, both as an engineer and as an athlete.

When I was initially employed, my fuel, fire, blaze was to prove to myself and to the organization that I had what it takes to succeed. I had to overcome the perception of my ability and the learning curve in order to make this happen. My fire goals were first, to meet all my key objectives, and second, to have time left over to bring innovative ideas to the table to facilitate the advancement of our products and our company. My fuel was to cultivate greater day-to-day productivity, so that I would have time to invest in industry research.

My axioms are as follows:

EVERY ACTION WE TAKE SETS A PRECEDENT
FOR OUR FOLLOWING ACTIONS.

Every decision counts. This eliminates the justification "just this once." Allowing a deadline to slip once sets a precedent that the next deadline can slip. Missing a workout sets a precedent that the next workout can be skipped. We must first be accountable to ourselves. One of my first battles as an engineer was communicating the value of sending status reports. I thought it was obvious, but I quickly realized that people don't know what you're challenged by or succeeding at if no one tells them. And who do you expect will tell them if you don't? Cultivating a habit of sending regular, concise updates helped me manage my career.

A good habit starts now. When things aren't gelling the way you think they should, that is the time to start a new healthy habit. Creating a habit takes the willpower of decision making out of the equation. This leaves you with plenty of energy left over to invest in other areas. When you are feeling bogged down on the job, determine one habit that will help you protect the resource of your own personal energy and move forward.

Who do you want to be? So many of our actions are determined by what we assume about ourselves. When I first began working at Microsoft, I would have readily admitted that I was disorganized—I would have said that it was an attribute that I had been born with and had no control over, and I would have said this with conviction.

Take control over the things that you have control over. Raise your own standards. If you are disorganized today but you hope to become organized tomorrow, the way you perceive yourself is the first battle. I want to be an organized person, so starting now, I am organized. Remember to set the bar high with regard to the person you want to be.

It was by adopting these axioms that I have been able to excel. Improving your habits takes constant dedication and self-awareness. Cultivating ever-increasing positive habits is like burning more efficient energy. This practice has enabled me to take on blaze goals of ever-increasing significance and impact. Today, I am confident that I do not know the upper limit of my potential. I know that if I continue to increase this premium of energy, I can have a tremendous positive impact on the world around me.

••• LESSONS •••

- Strengthen your willpower by cultivating healthy habits.
- To influence positive change in your life, establish motivation, monitor your behavior toward your goals, and use willpower to implement positive changes.
- Create a purposeful habit by selecting a behavior that will push you toward your blaze goals, then commit to doing this behavior for the 21 days required to make it automatic. Celebrate your success when your new, purposeful behavior becomes a habit.
- Keep your chosen behaviors simple. Do what is within your control right now.

CHAPTER 11

THE ROAD AHEAD

. . . .

What a blessed life I have! In my time of need, an army of supporters came to my rescue. I have had countless opportunities to achieve beyond my wildest aspirations. I used to feel that I was second class. I used to feel that I had something to prove to the world and, more important, to myself. Today, I feel only excitement about all that is possible. I feel only the spirit of adventure as I explore a limitless upward trajectory. I know that many more opportunities to demonstrate my resilience will come, and I understand that my life will never be free of challenge, but how exciting it is to know that each time I face adversity, I have the opportunity to discover new talents and ability. I do not fear risk. I embrace the opportunity to push myself further.

One thing I've realized—experienced up close and personal—over the past couple of years is that being a high-level athlete at the top of her game takes more than physical strength and mental toughness. While those are certainly important parts of the equation, we require one more thing in large quantities: business smarts.

Running an athletic campaign is very much like running a small business. To represent the United States internationally, at any level, is a privilege. Being an athlete renewed my sense of patriotism—there is no greater honor than wearing the uniform of your country. The not-so-dirty secret about athletics—even at the amateur level—is that it can be a very expensive proposition for those who engage in it.

Turning athletics into a business is not for the faint of heart. As with any business, the first step is to cover your costs. For blind athletes like me, the cost is double: in addition to my own travel, lodging, and food expenses for my competitions, I am also responsible for the travel, lodging, and food expenses of my guides.

When I raced in Auckland, New Zealand, where I won my second International Triathlon Union (ITU) bronze metal, I had landed a sponsorship that promised to help me cover my expenses. There was just one problem: it was conditional upon my placing on the podium. The water was a breathtaking 53 degrees, and I was tethered to Angie Balentine—an amazing guide and swimmer. I was worried that I would panic, but I knew that even if I did, I was in good hands. The whistle blew and the race began. I did not panic, but the athlete to my right did. She grabbed my leg, then my waist, and finally my throat. All I could think was, "Why are you hurting me?!"

Fortunately, Angie had her wits about her enough to yell into the water, "You're fine!!" I heard her words through the chaos, and I knew she was right. I ducked out from under this girl, pried her fingers loose, and freed myself. I immediately remembered that if I didn't place in the top three, I was out the money for both of us to travel to New Zealand—in the neighborhood of $10,000. That was all the motivation I needed to get my head back on straight.

I was second to last out of the water, and I knew that I'd have to make up time on the bike and the run. Thankfully, we passed a lot of competitors and came in fifth on the bike. We were then able to run down two athletes and take third place. I have never worked harder than I did for that bronze metal.

The pressure to perform as an athlete is key, as there are always associated costs and opportunities. Your opportunities to lose money are boundless, as are your opportunities to make money in the form of sponsorships and commitments to support other brands, which come largely in the form of performance bonuses. For example, for athletes sponsored by PowerBar, as I am, there is a negotiated cash prize for placing on the podium if I wear the PowerBar logo on my uniform. This is a typical agreement. As an athlete sponsored by the Challenged Athletes Foundation elite team, the travel expenses for myself and my guide are paid for by the foundation. This is a key piece, as it enables me to spend less money and to take advantage of opportunities to compete internationally. As I move closer to the 2016 Rio Paralympics, I will follow in the steps of athletes I have seen before me and take a position coaching triathlon for TriDot, which has developed a unique triathlon training system. The advantage of coaching is an increased knowledge base in your sport, the ability to work from home, and flexible hours to accommodate training and rest.

The governing bodies for Olympic and Paralympic sports have complicated structures. One thing most people don't know is that the Olympics are entirely privately funded—not a penny of federal money goes into supporting the U.S. Olympic and Paralympic teams. Key funders include McDonald's, 24-Hour Fitness, and United Airlines. The governing body is the U.S. Olympic Committee (USOC), and each sport has a federation within the USOC. For triathlon, this is the U.S. Association of Triathlon (USAT), and within the USAT there is a division for paratriathlon. The USOC partners with the International Paralympic Committee (IPC) and the ITU to govern the sport's inclusion in the Paralympics. All this is to say that there are opportunities for athletes to receive funding through their federations.

The opportunity for tiered funding based on performance was introduced in paratriathlon at the USAT level. This is a monthly stipend for expenses, coaching benefits, and, most important, health insurance. God willing, they will have a residency program for paratriathlon at the U.S. Olympic Training Center. In the event that they have a residency program, coaching, food, housing, and facilities will all be covered. Everything you need to live and thrive is there at the training center, which frees you up to focus your effort fully on becoming the best athlete you can be.

Opportunities for winning prize money in paratriathlon are few and far between. There are, however, an increasing number of other opportunities. For example, the Accenture Challenged Athletes International Championship in New York City has a prize for percentage of improvement over benchmark time for your category. In the summer of 2013, I competed against my own benchmark time at the New York City Triathlon. I did in fact win the prize, which came in the form of a giant check, the kind you see awarded to lottery winners on TV. My guide had already taken off, and I was left on my own to navigate the streets of New York City, with my cane, bike box, triathlon bag, laptop, and this huge check.

I made it all the way to JFK airport, where I checked in, frazzled from the stress of navigating the streets of New York and exhausted from the race. To be clear, navigating the streets of New York City as a blind person *without* a load is difficult enough, but add in two armloads of gear and that big check, and you've got a recipe for certain frenzy.

I made it to the gate, only to be approached by an athlete whom I have a bit of an adversarial relationship with. She walked up to me and asked if I was sentimental.

I said, "No, not particularly."

"So, what are you doing with that check?"

I replied, "Well, I'm taking it to the bank, obviously."

The woman laughed hysterically—I was the butt of her joke. You don't take the huge cardboard check to the bank—they send you a regular check in the mail. I had no idea. So I left that check at JFK airport; for all I know, it may still be there. My competitor went on to tell everyone at the gate, and I know I brought a lot of joy to a lot of people that day. They started writing me million-dollar checks on whatever they had handy: a coffee cup, a stick of gum, the back of a magazine. I can imagine that this would pale, however, in comparison to the laughter I would have heard had I walked into my local Chase bank branch with my giant check.

To make a long story short, it isn't easy to make money as an athlete, much less as an amateur athlete like myself. Most of us nickel-and-dime it together until we at least break even—or get as close as we can. Regardless of the potential financial and opportunity losses that we incur, however, the honor of representing our country is always worth it. I have traveled in the developing world enough to have a genuine appreciation for our freedoms. I have loved ones who have fought for my country and made tremendous sacrifices, like my personal hero, U.S. paratriathlete and Iraq War veteran Melissa Stockwell. I am nothing but proud to be American.

It happened that 2013 was a year of heartbreak for me—one that made me wonder why I had set my goals so high, and whether I would ever achieve them.

I had an incredible guide in Kerry Spearing. We had been training hard, and we entered the world championship with a first-place ranking. My swim has always been my most troubled discipline, so in 2013, I had spent endless hours focused on improving it. It was Friday the thirteenth in London—if I hadn't been superstitious before, I certainly was after. We were on our way to the race on our tandem bike when we came across construction on the bike path, so we decided to go off-road on the wet grass. Big mistake! We crashed to the ground, and poor Kerry fractured her shoulder (we didn't find out that she had fractured it until five weeks later). Once we got to the line to set up our gear for the race, I realized that I had mistaken a neoprene cap for my wet suit, and Kerry had to run back to get my suit. We were now rushing, which hampered our mental game. I felt awful and embarrassed at making such a rookie move. But we made it to the start, and we still felt confident in our ability to win the race.

In 2011, I had been last out of the water. In 2012, I did slightly better, being second from the last. In 2013, however, we were second out of the water, which meant a major improvement. We tore through the transition from swimming to biking and were first out of the transition and now leading on the bike. What I was most proud of was how well we were working together. For a tandem bike to really work, each rider has to put exactly the same amount of power and cadence into it—the same everything. People are forever trying to make the case to me that riding tandem is an advantage. I don't always say it, but in the back of my mind I think about the old joke that a tandem is a "divorce maker." It is extremely hard to get two people working in exact synchronicity with decent power output.

Kerry and I were accelerating together, leaning together—we were clearly one team. The day of the race, there was a drizzling rain on the cobblestones that made up the road surface. We had just lapped our closest competitor with three miles to go on the bike. Both Kerry and I are runners at heart, so I knew that the second we got off the bike and hit the run, we had the world championship. I took comfort in knowing that my family was watching online and thrilled that my coworkers were all watching as well. I was daydreaming about how I might be received on my return—a champion's welcome.

Clearly, I had become overconfident.

Sure enough, we got the first and only flat tire of my entire career. In a split second, the 2013 world championship went from being the best race of my life to the worst. It went from imagining my hero's reception to genuine sadness that everyone saw one of my lowest, most disappointing moments. I had trained for years to lead a world championship race, and my hopes were foiled by a pebble that had punctured my tube.

In that moment, as we racked our brains to come up with some sort of solution, I realized that I am a person who speaks to thousands of people every year about what it is to fail gracefully. I knew in that instant that as gut-wrenching as this loss was for me, it was an opportunity to practice what I preach. This was a failure that was caused by things that were outside of my control. Inherent in all pursuits are some risks, but with high risk comes the potential for high reward or tremendous failure.

Kerry was a champion. She was down to earth and calm throughout the ordeal, and I tried to present my best self. I called my Aunt Janet because I had no idea what to do and felt that my disappointment was getting the better of me. As always, she gave me sage advice: "Well, a few hours ago you were a Paralympic-bound athlete, and now you are an Oscar award–winning actress. Go win your award!" What she meant was, go to the postrace events, go to the awards ceremony, and muster the most sincerity possible. When the disappointment trumps the sincerity, then fake it like an Oscar-winning actress. You cannot control how you feel, but you can always control how you act.

I took it on as a personal challenge to be the picture of graciousness and good sportsmanship. I probably landed somewhere halfway between the two opposing extremes of how I actually felt and how I wanted to project myself to the world.

After the disappointing 2013 world championship, I had a renewed hunger to win. I know that there is no workout that can prepare you for a flat tire. That said, I still felt outclassed during the race. I came home aching for a more structured, more demanding program. I had been burdened with injury and fatigue, and people kept telling me that I had more in me. I also felt that I had more in me, but I had no idea how to plumb those depths. I went on to interview several coaches in and outside of Austin, Texas, some even as far away as Canada.

I love Austin, and I have never felt so at home in my life as I do in Austin, but I knew that I had to be willing to relocate if my future coach, whoever it was that I decided would be the *best* coach for me, wasn't in Austin. I felt that I had already invested so much time and energy at this point that a new location and more money was a small price to pay. As an athlete, it is your responsibility to arm yourself with the right tools. I wouldn't run without good shoes. Why would it make sense to train without the best guidance possible?

Thank God the best coach in the country for me just happened to be in Austin! I had met Natasha Van Der Merwe before, but I had been misinformed about her swimming style. I loved that she had her core values—"God, Family, Husband, Triathlon"—on her website for all to see. Everything about Natasha seemed right, and I was certain that she was the missing piece I needed to dig a little deeper and get more out of myself. Sure enough, she introduced some structure into my program, including adding more sleep and timing my restrictive diet. I started enjoying my training more every day, and I began seeing monster gains in all disciplines.

After the heartbreak of 2013, I seriously entertained the thought of walking away from the sport. Training is a lot of work, and I feel that I've sacrificed a lot. To keep myself going, I remind myself of everything that has gone into this and of all the naysayers I've surprised along the way. I remind myself of all those long years as a marathoner and the many athletes who didn't even know that there were blind athletes. If I can use any of that experience to help others, disabled or otherwise, achieve their full potential, then it will all have been worthwhile.

People always told me that I had more, but I felt as if I was beating my head against a wall trying to become more. Clearly, training more wasn't the answer, and being more disciplined wasn't the answer either. The answer was training *smarter*, and Natasha offered me the tools to do that.

Even though your challenges may not be in the realm of athletics, I feel that the lessons I've learned from my journey are applicable to any battle you may be fighting—the challenge to tap into your inner strength and sense of ability. I feel it is my responsibility to share these tools with others who are struggling with their own personal challenges in life. I encourage all of you to invest in your core values and cultivate your own conviction. A life of limitless upward potential is exciting.

Fighting *with* conviction is like swimming with the river, while fighting *without* conviction is like swimming against the current. Choose to make your life easier for yourself by fighting with conviction.

I intend to spend the coming years practicing what I preach. I have proved to myself that a downward spiral knows no boundaries—things can *always* get worse; there truly is no bottom to how low you can go. But if things can always get worse, then it follows that things can always get better. I live to prove that that upward trajectory also knows no bounds.

Where I once stood with no lifeline, today I stand with an army of supporters. I know that with each incident, with each trial and tribulation, I become that much more capable. I know that when I do need help, which I inevitably will, that help will come. From where I'm standing, the road ahead may certainly hold some surprises, but the future is looking bright.

In 2002, when I ran my first mile, I had no idea of the cause and effect that was beginning. With each step forward, I set in motion a process that moved me ever closer to having a better life. First, I became less scared. I unlearned my learned helplessness. Then I became more fit. Once I was more fit, I started having incremental successes in athletics. Once I had a few successes under my belt, I enjoyed improved self-esteem and a greater desire to succeed. Improved self-esteem motivated me to take on ever-increasing challenges. This continually building trajectory of the positive led me to lead a life beyond my wildest dreams. I am far happier and more fulfilled now than I ever dreamed was possible. Even when I find myself in a position that tests my resilience, even when I find myself in those inevitable lows, my life is still better than I could ever have hoped. When I had lost my home, lost everything, and was facing my dad's deteriorating health, my life was full of kindnesses, opportunities, and blessings. I believe in myself in all situations, and this belief carries me through anything. Cultivate your own sense of self. Take on your ability to achieve as a responsibility starting today.

I look forward to representing my country in 2016 at the Paralympics in Rio de Janeiro, God willing, and here's hoping that I will bring home a gold medal for my country, my family, my coaches, and all who have supported me along the way. I invite the naysayers to celebrate with me, as were it not for their pessimism, I probably wouldn't have pushed as hard.

My fuel is my tools, technology, supporters, and the drive that make the day-to-day exercises possible. My ongoing fire is my next international opportunity to represent my country. My blaze is to make my country and my family proud. My blaze is to live as an example of what is possible, so that others will be inspired and live with a sense of what may be possible in their own lives. With the fuel, fire, blaze hierarchy, I have exceeded my wildest dreams. I hope to help unleash others to live with that same enchanting sense of ability.

My hope for you is that you feel a renewed sense of empowerment for your own blaze goals. I stress for a final time that the only thing that matters is that these goals are important to you on an emotional, authentic level. Embrace the motivation that you have at your fingertips by preparing yourself with the tools you need if you are to be successful.

My greatest aspiration today is that each of you feels empowered to overcome your own self-doubt, to quiet your naysayers. I hope each of you feels capable of pushing yourself a little harder, trying to operate at a level where you are always just about to hit the wall. I hope each of you feels ever more excited about living to your full potential and the boundless upward trajectory you could begin today. I pray that each of you feels inspired to approach each day with a renewed appetite for your own blind ambition.

ENDNOTES

CHAPTER 2

1. Ad Kleingeld, Heleen van Mierlo, and Lidia Arends, "The Effect of Goal Setting on Group Performance: A Meta-Analysis," Journal of Applied Psychology 96, no. 6 (2011), pp. 1289–1304, cited in Sebastian Bailey, "The Truth About Goals," Forbes, October 2, 2012; http://www.forbes.com/sites/sebastianbailey/2012/10/02/the-truth-about-goals/.
2. Gail Matthews, "Study Backs Up Strategies for Achieving Goals," News Room, Dominican University of California; http://www.dominican.edu/dominicannews/study-backs-up-strategies-for-achieving-goals.
3. Jim Collins and Jerry Porras, Built to Last: Successful Habits of Visionary Companies (New York: HarperBusiness, 1994).
4. W. Erickson, C. Lee, and S. von Schrader, Disability Statistics from the 2012 American Community Survey (ACS) (Ithaca, NY: Cornell University Employment and Disability Institute, 2014), cited in National Foundation of the Blind, "Blindness Statistics"; https://nfb.org/blindness-statistics.

CHAPTER 3

1. Abigail Flesch Connors, Teaching Creativity: Supporting, Valuing, and Inspiring Young Children's Creative Thinking (Pittsburgh: Whitmore Publishing, 2010) p. xii
2. "Highest High Jump (Female)," Guinness World Records; http://www.guinnessworldrecords.com/records-11000/highest-high-jump-(female)/.
3. U.S. Bureau of Labor Statistics, Business Employment Dynamics, summarized in U.S. Small Business administration, Office of Advocacy, "Do Economic or Industry Factors Affect Business Survival?," Small Business Facts, June 2012, cited in Resources for Entrepreneurs; http://www.gaebler.com/Small-Business-Failure-Rates.htm.

CHAPTER 4

1. Angela Duckworth, "Research Statement," The Duckworth Lab, University of Pennsylvania; https://sites.sas.upenn.edu/duckworth/pages/research.
2. Angela Duckworth, "The Key to Success? Grit," TED Talks, May 2013; http://www.ted.com/talks/angela_lee_duckworth_the_key_to_success _grit/transcript.
3. Hazel Symonette, "Make Assessment Work for You and Your Student Success Vision: It Works if You Work It!," 2013 Institute on Integrative Learning and the Departments, Association of American Colleges and Universities, July 10–14. 2013; https://www.aacu.org/meetings/ild /documents/Symonette.MakeAssessmentWork.Dweck.pdf.
4. Margaret Perlis, "5 Characteristics of Grit—How Many Do You Have?," Forbes, October 19, 2013; http://www.forbes.com/sites/margaretperlis /2013/10/29/5-characteristics-of-grit-what-it-is-why-you-need-it-and -do-you-have-it/.

CHAPTER 5

1. "Too Many Interruptions at Work?," Gallup Business Journal, June 8, 2006; http://businessjournal.gallup.com/content/23146/too-many-interruptions -work.aspx.
2. Sarah Green, "The Myth of Monotasking," Harvard Business Review, November 23, 2011; http://blogs.hbr.org/2011/11/the-myth-of -monotasking/.
3. David Woodward, "Research Claims Social Media Costs Millions in Lost Productivity," Director, 2014; http://www.director.co.uk/ONLINE/2011 /05_11_social_media_productivity.html.
4. "I Can't Get My Work Done! How Collaboration and Social Tools Drain Productivity," harmon.ie, May 18, 2011, p. 2; http://harmon.ie/Downloads /DistractionSurveyResults.
5. Cheryl Conner, "Employees Really Do Waste Time at Work," Forbes, November 15, 2012; http://www.forbes.com/sites/cherylsnappconner /2012/11/15/employees-really-do-waste-time-at-work-part-ii/.
6. Anne Fisher, "The Three Biggest Workplace Distractions," Fortune, June 12, 2013; http://fortune.com/2013/06/12/the-three-biggest-workplace -distractions/.
7. Issie Lapowsky, "Don't Multitask: Your Brain Will Thank You," Inc., April 8, 2013; http://www.inc.com/magazine/201304/issie-lapowsky/get-more -done-dont-multitask.html

CHAPTER 6

1. Albert Ellis, How to Make Yourself Happy and Remarkably Less Disturbable (Atascadero: Impact Publishers, 1999) p. 8.
2. Brandon Gaille, "17 Lazy Procrastination Statistics," BrandonGaille .com, December 13, 2013; http://brandongaille.com/17-lazy -procrastination-statistics/.
3. Amy Spencer, "The Science Behind Procrastination," Real Simple; http://www.realsimple.com/work-life/life-strategies/time-management /procrastination-00000000055281/.

CHAPTER 7

1. Sasha Galbraith, "Bayer CropScience's Sandra Peterson: Successful Woman CEO Navigates in a Man's World," Forbes, December 7, 2011; http:// www.forbes.com/sites/sashagalbraith/2011/12/07/bayer-cropsciences -sandra-peterson-successful-ceo-navigates-in-a-mans-world/.
2. Peter Sims, Little Bets: How Breakthrough Ideas Emerge from Small Discoveries (New York: Simon & Schuster, 2011), p. 53.

CHAPTER 8

1. Tony Hsieh, "How Zappos Infuses Culture Using Core Values," HBR Blog Network, May 24, 2010; http://blogs.hbr.org/2010/05/how-zappos -infuses-culture-using-core-values/.
2. Delivering Happiness; http://deliveringhappiness.com/work/.
3. Great Place to Work Institute, "What Are the Benefits?"; http://www .greatplacetowork.com/our-approach/what-are-the-benefits-great -workplaces.

CHAPTER 9

1. "Business Resilience—Anticipation as the Key to Sustainable Business Success," European Foundation for the Improvement of Living and Working Conditions, Noordwijk, the Netherlands, June 2–3, 2004; http://www.eurofound.europa.eu/emcc/content/source/eu04021a.htm ?p1=reports&p2=null.
2. "Business Resilience: The Best Defense Is a Good Offense," IBM Business Continuity and Resiliency Services, January 2009; http://www .ibm.com/smarterplanet/global/files/us__en_us__security_resiliency__ buw03008usen.pdf.

3. DiscoveryHealth.com, "10 Ways to Build Resilience," HowStuffWorks; http://health.howstuffworks.com/mental-health/coping/ten-ways-to-build-resilience.htm#page=0.

CHAPTER 10
1. "What You Need to Know About Willpower: The Psychological Science of Self-Control," American Psychological Association, p. 6; http://www.apa.org/helpcenter/willpower.aspx, accessed April 7, 2014.
2. Ibid.
3. Ibid., p. 7.

INDEX

About the Author

Diagnosed with a pediatric brain tumor, Patricia Walsh became partially blind at the age of 5. As a teenager, she lost what little vision remained due to surgical complications, and struggled with depression and hopelessness. Today, Walsh is a world champion paratriathlete and an award-winning engineer. She has raced in more than a dozen marathons and ultra-marathons and competed in two IRONMAN triathlons. In 2011, she set the world record for blind triathletes, shattering both male and female records by over 50 minutes.

Patricia Walsh has a bachelor's degree in computer science and electrical engineering from Oregon State University and a master's degree in executive nonprofit leadership from Seattle University. She was one of the first blind engineers at Microsoft. She is the 2011, 2012, and 2013 paratriathlon national champion; the 2012 PATCO Pan American champion; a winner in the 2014 PATCO Pan American; and a bronze medalist at both the 2011 and 2012 ITU World Championships. She is a member of the U.S. Paratriathlon National Team and aspires to represent her country at the 2016 Paralympic Games in Rio de Janeiro, Brazil.

Patricia Walsh is the founder and owner of Blind Ambition LLC, a speaking and business consultancy that specializes in goal achievement keynotes, as well as seminars on the topics of goal achievement, overcoming obstacles, leadership, creating a winning mindset, and team building.

She lives in Austin, Texas.

Visit her website at www.blindambitionspeaking.com and follow her on Twitter at @BlindAmbitionSp.